The Gardening Gamble

The Gardening Gamble

Heather Reimer

Betty Yung

The Gardening Gamble

KEY PORTER BOOKS

Library and Archives Canada Cataloguing in Publication

Reimer, heather
        The gardening gamble / Heater Reimer, Betty Yung.

ISBN 1-55263-652-6

        1. Gardens--Design.   2.Landscape gardening,
I. yung, Betty II. Title.

SB473.R45 2005   712' .6   C2005-900134-8

The publisher gratefully acknowledges the support of the Canada Council for the Arts and the Ontario Arts Council for its publishing program. We acknowledge the support of the Government of Ontario through the Ontario Media Development Corporation's Ontario Book Initiative.

We acknowledge the financial support of the Government of Canada through the Book Publishing Industry Development Program (BPIDP) for our publishing activities.

Key Porter Books Limited
Six Adelaide Street East,
Tenth Floor,
Toronto, Ontario
Canada M5C 1H6

www.keyporter.com

Text design/formatting: Jack Steiner

Illustration: Carrie Chisholm (p. 130), John Lightfoot (p. 132)

Photogaphy: Tanja-Tiziana Burdi, Jay Moeller, Heather Reimer, Donabel Joy Santos, Jen Thompson, Mark Trutnau, AaRon van Borek, and Betty Yung

Printed and bound in Canada

05 06 07 08 09 5 4 3 2 1

Table of Contents

Color My Garden

The Challenge

Rob and Robin Barbara have had the title of "homeowners" for just over a year. They said they lacked vision when it came to designing their yard and hoped *The Gardening Gamble* experts could put them on the right track. They had a traditional square yard with weedy gardens, an old garage and a concrete pathway bordering the space. The lack of privacy and concrete throughout the yard were the two biggest complaints from the Barbaras. They rarely used the yard because they thought it was unattractive.

Rob and Robin Barbara

The Goal

To create a functional and private space where the Barbaras could entertain and dine with friends.

The Solution

The first thing landscape professional Edgar Friars wanted to do in this space was create a focal point. He envisioned a central seating area surrounded by gardens. Edgar wanted the yard to be a "learning garden" for Rob and Robin so that they could have the foundation of a blooming garden for the future. He decided to plant in themes: a fragrant garden, a bird garden, and an edible-flower garden. The concrete path was removed, and the concrete paving stones went to the center of the lawn to create the new seating area. A coat of blue paint brightened up the shed, and privacy panels enclosed the seating area.

A Garden for the Birds

Birds are a perfect accompaniment to your garden. Attracting them is as simple as providing them with what they need. A bird garden should provide food, shelter and a water source such as a pond or birdbath. Your garden can have a mix of plant material that's attractive to both you and birds. When selecting plants for your garden, consider what types of birds you'd like to attract. You can attract a multitude of birds with berry-producing shrubs such as (from top to bottom) Viburnum (Viburnum), Golden Japanese Barberry (Berberis thunbergii 'Aurea') and Chokeberry (Aronia). Check with your local ornithological association to find other bird-favorite plants.

The Projects

- Transplanting a mature bush or tree
- Planting a fragrant garden

The Budget

Plant material	$ 960.00
Screening and soil	$ 210.00
Carpentry	$ 295.00
Accessories/paint	$ 490.00
Total	**$1955.00**

AFTER

BEFORE

AFTER: Color, plants and privacy are just what Edgar ordered.

BEFORE (inset): A basic yard lacking any character.

The Plan

Replanting a Mature Bush or Tree

Edgar planted a mature **forsythia bush** (*Forsythia x intermedia*) as a focal point to his "learning garden." It provided instant interest and privacy from the neighbors. The forsythia bush thrives in sunny areas with well-drained soil. It has showy yellow flowers in early spring and grows 8 to 10 feet (2.44 to 3 m) tall. A hardy landscaping favorite, it's best for USDA Zone 5. Unless you're redesigning your yard or have inherited a mature bush, it's unlikely you'll be able to purchase one from your local nursery. But if you do get your hands on one, here's how to replant it once you get it home.

What you will need:

- Shovel
- Transplanting solution
- Garden hose/water
- Mulch

1. Dig a hole at the new planting site. The hole should be three times wider than and as deep as the rootball.

2. Gently place the shrub in the hole. Ensure that it's standing straight and begin backfilling the hole. Tamp the soil to prevent air holes, and water with a transplanting solution as you go. The solution will help establish a new root system.

3. When the hole is filled, mound up the soil in a ring around the base so that it forms a well to catch water. This will keep the roots moist. Cover the soil at the base with at least 3 inches (7.5 cm) of mulch to help retain moisture to the root area.

4. Water often! The first year will be very difficult for the shrub to weather unless it gets plenty to drink.

NOTE: It's best to replant when the shrub is dormant, in fall or winter. It's not ideal to replant during the summer, when the plant's metabolism is high, but not impossible. You can keep the shrub out of the ground and delay replanting as long as the roots remain wet. Wrapping the roots in mulch and burlap will help with this.

Planting a Fragrant Garden

A fragrant garden will look and smell beautiful, and with the right mix, you can enjoy various scents all year long. Here are some things to keep in mind when planting a fragrant garden:

- **LOCATION**—You'll enjoy the garden more if it's in the right spot. Edgar planted the garden close to a house window as well as next to the seating area so that Robin and Rob can enjoy the scents inside and out.

- **AMOUNT OF LIGHT**—A sunny yard is ideal. The heat will help release and intensify scents, so you get more enjoyment out of the plants.

- **PLANT MIX**—You can create an interesting blend of scents depending on the type of plants you choose. Pick plants with scents that compliment rather than overpower each other.

- Remember, the more fragrant the plant, the more insects it will attract. If bugs bug you, this garden might not be for you.

DESIGN PLAN

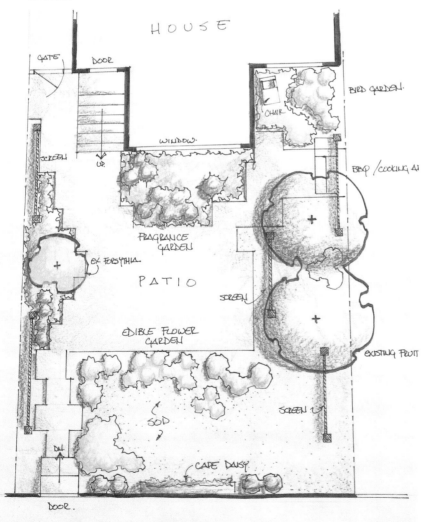

LOCATION—be sure to place your plants where you'll enjoy their fragrance.

AMOUNT OF LIGHT—full sun is the best condition to fully enjoy your fragrant garden.

PLANT MIX—Edgar sets out his plant choices to see where they look and smell best.

The Plants

The plant material Edgar selected for the learning garden was suited to the yard's sunny space.

Fragrant Garden

■ **Sweet Alyssum (*Lobularia maritima*)** This delicate annual packs a lot of punch for its size. It produces an abundance of blooms in spring but grows to less than a foot (30 cm) tall. The flowers have a honey-like scent. White flowers are the most fragrant. Pinch off old blooms to extend the blooming period. Fast-growing, the plant thrives in full to part sun. Use in borders, containers or rock gardens.

■ **'Snowbelle' Mock Orange** (*Philadelphus x virginalis* **'Snowbelle'**) is a great choice for a fragrant garden, this shrub has blooms of fragrant semi-double white flowers in late spring. A compact grower, its mature height is 4–5 feet (1.2–1.5 m) tall, and it likes sun to partial shade. Pruning the mock orange is the key to new flowers the following season; be sure to prune it right after flowering. A hardy shrub, it's ideal for USDA Zones 5-8.

Other plants Edgar included were:

■ **Chinese Lilac (*Syringa x chinensis* 'Saugeana')**

■ **French Hybrid Lilac (*Syringa vulgaris* 'French Hybrid')**

■ **German Bearded Iris 'Superstition' (*Iris germanica* 'Superstition')**

■ **Peony (*Paeonia*)**

The Result

Rob and Robin said they wanted privacy in their yard, and Edgar certainly delivered. The colorful panels and the forsythia frame their new focal point—a dining and entertaining area. Let the party begin!

Sweet Alyssum

'Snowbelle' Mock Orange

Chinese Lilac

French Hybrid Lilac

German Bearded Iris

Peony

A Shady Deal

The Challenge

Kate Skillicorn and David Bradley felt their yard was boring, but their gardening know-how was limited. After trying to put down new sod a few times with little success and planting a few flowers, they ran out of steam.

The concrete deck near the house was shady and uninviting. In fact, shade was a problem in most of the garden. The yard was narrow and lacked any landscape structures or architectural detail, and an old concrete pathway ran through the middle of the garden. It was crying out for an interesting plan, and they hoped their "gamble" would pay off.

David Bradley and Kate Skillicorn

The Goal

To turn this shady garden into a more useable space by creating several unique 'rooms' within the backyard—making it feel warm, friendly and inviting.

The Solution

Landscape designer Cathy Merklinger wanted to make a statement in this bland backyard. She felt a shade garden needed to feel brighter. To achieve this, she incorporated hits of bright color with plants and accessories. Since the garden was long and narrow, she felt that dividing it up into several sections or rooms would break up the space nicely.

The Budget

Plant materials	$ 675.00
Carpentry (deck, pergola, stone materials)	$ 645.00
Accessories—table, chairs, planters, urns	$ 500.00
Soil, screenings	$ 140.00
TOTAL (excluding paint)	**$1960.00**

Made in the Shade

The term "partial shade" refers to a garden that gets less than 5 hours of direct sunlight per day. "Full sun" refers to gardens that get more than 3 hours of direct sun per day, while "full shade" describes a garden that receives no direct sunlight.

The amount of sunlight an area receives will change with the seasons. Also, as trees mature, gardens often become shadier.

A shade garden is not necessarily a bad thing. Shade gardens attract fewer insects and provide a nice retreat from the scorching sun. As well, moisture evaporates more quickly from a sunny spot, so less watering is required in a shade garden. Many people complain that nothing will grow in their shaded yard. However, contrary to popular belief, there are many attractive shrubs, flowers and groundcovers that thrive in the shade.

ROOM 1: A fun, bright space to relax and barbecue.

ROOM 2: A tranquil area with a lush groundcover.

ROOM 3: A deck and pergola, complete with table and chairs for an elegant dining area.

ROOM 4: A whimsical room. Since the homeowners were young, hip teachers, Cathy added an old school desk as a focal point.

The Projects

- Constructing a stone walkway
- Planting groundcovers

AFTER: Separate areas break up the long garden. Bright colors add drama and interest to the space.

BEFORE (inset): Long and narrow, this garden was a cold and uninviting space, with no appeal.

The Plan

Constructing a Stone Walkway

Stonework adds a natural touch to a garden and can increase your property value. Interlocking stones are a great option for both esthetic appeal and durability. They are up to four times stronger than poured concrete, less likely to crack and very flexible in extreme temperatures. Building a stone walkway can be time-consuming (depending on the size of the walkway and the stones), but the results are worth the effort. To determine how much material you will need, consult your local landscape-supply store.

Materials you will need:

- Rake
- Shovel
- Tamper
- Level
- Mallet
- Broom
- Limestone screenings
- Interlocking stones
- Sand

1. Prepare your surface by removing sod and raking ground. Excavate 3 inches (7.5 cm) for limestone screenings.
2. Use a hand or machine tamper to compress the surface.
3. Make sure the ground is level or graded slightly for water runoff away from the house.
4. Spread 3-5 inches (7.5-12.5 cm) of limestone screening along area. Tamp and level screenings.
5. Lay stones in place, using a mallet to set each stone onto the limestone base.
6. Spread sand on top of stone walkway and use a broom to sweep it into the cracks. The sand will bond the bricks together for a strong, long-lasting walkway.

Planting Groundcovers

Groundcovers are a great alternative to grass. The homeowners had tried three times to lay sod in their shade garden and weren't having much success. Where grass won't grow is where a groundcover will most likely thrive. Groundcovers are low-maintenance plants that look great and help control weeds. Besides, they spread quickly. We used the popular Pachysandra (*Pachysandra terminalis*), which is ideal for shady locations. It tolerates any type of soil and is hardy in USDA Zones 4-8. It has thick, glossy green leaves and white flowers that bloom in May.

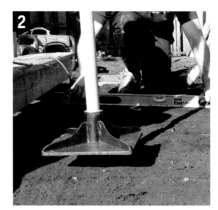

DESIGN PLAN

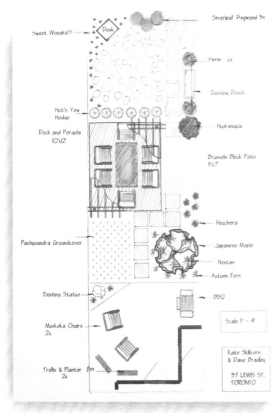

Materials you will need:

- Rake
- Trowel/shovel
- Measuring tape
- Plants

1. Prepare the area for planting by removing any sod, raking and leveling ground. Add compost if necessary. Using a trowel or shovel, dig holes to the appropriate depth so that the rootball sits just below the surface. Use a measuring tape if you are unsure.
2. Place one plant in each hole, holding the stem gently for support.
3. Backfill the soil firmly around the rootball. Water well.
4. Plants should be spaced about 12 inches (30 cm) apart, one plant per square foot (0.1 m²) For instant results, space plants 4 inches (10 cm) apart. Water daily until the roots take.

The Plants

The plants Cathy chose for the garden were all plants that would thrive in the shade. She wanted a combination of interesting texture and bright pink flowers.

- **Busy Lizzie Impatiens** (*Impatiens walleriana* '**Dazzler Deep Pink**') have striking pink blooms that matched perfectly with Cathy's color scheme. Potted in matching pink pots, they would dress up the barbecue area. Along with thriving in shade, they like moist, well-drained soil. They have only medium water requirements and bloom through summer and fall.

- **Japanese Maple** (*Acer palmatum*) is a wonderful addition to any garden. It is extremely hardy (USDA Zones 4-8) and has lovely reddish

leaves. It grows in full sun to partial shade in any well-drained soil and should be kept moist during the growing season.

- Again, the **Silverleaf Dogwood** (*Cornus alba* '**Elegantissima**') was chosen for its ability to thrive in partial shade to sun. This shrub has grey-green leaves with white margins, and its stems turn dark red in winter. It is hardy in USDA Zones 3-8 and likes moist, well-drained soil. It will grow 5-6 feet (1.5-2 m) tall and spread 4-6 feet (1.5-2 m) wide.

Busy Lizzie Impatiens

Japanese Maple

Silverleaf Dogwood

The Result

The transformation was a success. The garden was divided into four distinct areas, with a spectacular "dining room" as the centerpiece. The sod that wouldn't grow gave way to a lush groundcover that will fill in its "room" in no time. The narrow, dark garden was brightened up with funky accessories and pink flowers—perfect for a young urban couple.

Sunstroke

The Challenge

Sarah and Rob Fayle had been in their home for four years. Their backyard was a large grassy area enclosed by a 15-foot (4.6 m) cedar hedge. A small white shed sat in the middle of the yard. Aside from that, there was no structure in the garden.

A novice gardener, Sarah had maintained a couple of perennial beds next to the house with mixed success. Rob's job in the garden was trimming the large cedar hedge annually. The Fayles' biggest beef with their garden was too much sun, and nowhere to hide from it. Their kids loved to run amok in the yard, but the adults craved a nice patio for adult entertaining. With no time and no experience, they hoped *The Gardening Gamble* experts could give them what wanted.

Rob and Sarah Fayle

The Goal

To add structure, shade and striking colors to this boring garden.

The Solution

Landscape designer Cathy Merklinger met the Fayles and saw their dilemma. The yard was virtually a blank slate, and it lacked color. The white shed blended in with the house. She knew she had to incorporate shade, seating and structure into the space but wanted to include some interesting elements as well. She thought this young couple with children would appreciate a bold design. Three large umbrellas would address the shade issue, and some lounge chairs would add a secondary seating area. A new stone patio would become the foundation for a pergola with bench seats, providing more seating and structure. Bright blue and lime green were the colors chosen to electrify this dull space.

The garden beds were extended, and evergreen plants with height and textured foliage filled out the bed where there were existing perennials. This material would give year-round interest.

The Projects

- Creating a concrete paving-stone patio
- Planting Dwarf Korean Lilac Standards

The Budget

Plant materials	$ 436.00
Patio stones, screening, soil	$ 728.00
Accessories—chairs, cushions, umbrellas, art	$ 485.00
Carpentry (pergola)	$ 435.00
TOTAL	**$2084.00**

AFTER

BEFORE

AFTER: A proper seating area and pergola helped define this garden, while the bright color scheme is perfect for a sunny garden. Bold colors, umbrellas for shade and a proper patio were the keys to this garden transformation.

BEFORE (inset): This yard had healthy grass, a cute shed and that's about it.

The Plan

Creating a Concrete Paving-Stone Patio

The Fayles' garden needed structure and definition. Cathy had carpenter Lorne Hogan build a pergola with built-in seating, but it needed a foundation to rest on. She decided to go with a 14 × 18-foot (4.2 × 5.5 m) patio area, and the budget dictated that concrete paving stones were the best option. But Cathy did splurge on colored stones with a textured top. Instead of using limestone screenings as a base for the patio, she used a new material called quarterchip, otherwise known as high-performance bedding. This stone product is a washed limestone material that allows for free drainage and deters soil migration. It also requires less compaction, saving time and energy.

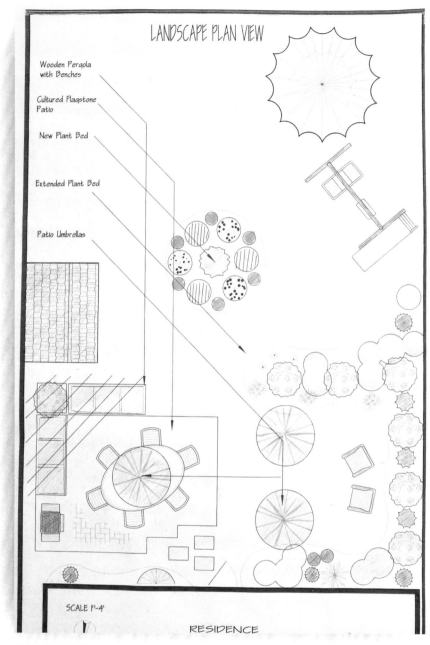

LANDSCAPE PLAN VIEW

Wooden Pergola
with Benches

Cultured Flagstone
Patio

New Plant Bed

Extended Plant Bed

Patio Umbrellas

SCALE 1"-4'

RESIDENCE

DESIGN PLAN

Materials you will need:

- Sharp-edged shovel
- Wheelbarrow
- Quarterchip patio base
- Level
- 4 foot (1.2 m) length of wood for leveling
- Concrete paving stones

1. Remove sod in patio area.
2. Dump and rake quarterchip to a depth of 2-3 inches (5-7.5 cm) on the entire surface.
3. Level quarterchip and tamp.
4. Place paving stones onto quarterchip surface in a random or tight-fitting pattern, as desired. Wiggle each stone to set into base. All paving stones should be level.

A patio and pergola give this yard a much-needed seating area.

Why Build Up?

A pergola or an arbor are great ways to add some height and structure to your space, as they add character and provide a focal point for decoration and design. Pergolas are great for vines, other climbing plants and hanging baskets. If you are still training your green thumb, try dressing up your pergolas with lights, ribbons or streamers for special occasions. We suspended art canvases to add some decoration and color to our white pergola. A pergola with benches, like the one Lorne built, had the added benefit of extra seating and storage—perfect for keeping cushions and table dressings dry and close at hand.

The finshed patio was a great base for the Fayles' outdoor dining area.

15

Planting Dwarf Korean Lilac Standards

Lilacs are native to Asia and Europe. They were brought to North America by French and Dutch colonists in the 18th century and have remained extremely popular ever since. They are a wonderful addition to any garden, as their strong fragrance permeates the air. There are over 1,000 varieties of lilac, with blooms in pink, lavender, blue, white and even yellow.

For the Fayles' garden, Cathy chose six **Dwarf Korean Lilac Standards** (*Syringa meyeri* 'Palabin'). She wanted to add some height to the garden beds, but not too much.

Dig a hole large enough to fit the rootball.

This native of Northern China thrives in full sun, although it will tolerate part shade. All lilacs require at least six hours of sunlight per day to bloom properly. The Dwarf Korean Lilac blooms profusely in spring and reflowers lightly in late summer to early fall. It produces powerfully fragrant lavender-pink flowers with green foliage, which turns bright yellow in fall. Unlike other common lilacs, this variety blooms a great deal at an early age and is not susceptible to powdery mildew. The standard version is

Place the shrub in the hole. The rootball should sit at the surface.

Backfill soil around the rootball. Pack firmly to eliminate any air pockets.

exceptionally charming, as it sits at average nose level, ensuring the full effect of its sweet scent.

It is extremely hardy, low-maintenance and easy to grow in USDA Zones 3-7. It reaches heights of up to 5 feet (1.5 m) tall and 7 feet (2 m) wide and tolerates most well-drained soil conditions.

When planting and caring for lilacs, here are some tips to keep in mind:

- Lilacs should not be planted too deep. The top surface of the soil ball should be level with the surrounding ground.
- Water three times per week for the first month. After that, water deeply once a week. The soil should also be well watered before the ground freezes in the fall. Do not overwater lilacs as they hate to have wet feet.
- Prune old blooms away immediately after flowering to encourage more blossoms.
- Do not fertilize the first year of planting. A general fertilizer or one high in phosphate to promote blooming can be applied in early spring in following years.

Hedge Your Bets

Hedges are a great way to create a natural fence for your yard. Hedges can keep people and animals in or out and provide shelter and privacy. The Fayles inherited a mature 15-foot (4.6 m) cedar hedge as a boundary for their garden. They loved the enclosed, natural feel it added to their yard.

Maintaining a natural fence does require some work, but the more informal your hedge is, the easier the task will be. When to trim back and by how much are good questions. You can trim any time of year, except when branches are frozen or during a summer hot spell. How much you trim depends on how quickly your hedge grows. If you are trimming to maintain height, most cedar hedges grow about 2 feet (60 cm) per year. You should trim at least once a year and may have to trim up to three times per year if growth is rapid.

Shape is important to maintaining a healthy hedge. It's best to aim for a tapered shape, narrower at the top than the base. This ensures that the sun will reach the entire hedge, and it helps shed snow in winter.

Whether you opt to go with gas, electric or manual tools, keeping them clean and sharp will make your task much easier and your tools will last much longer.

Hydrangea

shady spot. It thrives in shade to part-shade and is hardy in USDA Zones 4-8. White flowers bloom from spring to mid-summer against green and silver leaves.

- **Hydrangea (*Hydrangea paniculata* 'Brussels Lace')** is a vigorous shrub with dark green leaves that produces small panicles of creamy white flowers in summer that mature to pink and finally turn rusty-brown in fall. It thrives in full sun to partial shade and is adaptable to most soils, as long as they are well-drained. It is hardy in USDA Zones 4-8.

The Result

A large patio became home to a tall pergola with built-in benches to add much-needed height, structure and seating to the garden. It was also the perfect spot for family dining or adult entertaining. Several umbrellas were positioned around the garden to offer shelter from the sun as well as secondary seating areas. The shed was perked up with vibrant lime green and blue colors. This boring garden was now fun in the sun!

- Mulch can be used to keep roots cool and prevent weed growth, but do not suffocate the trunk with too much mulch.

Other Plants

Cathy chose various plants for the Fayles' garden. She wanted to add height, texture and color to this full-sun garden.

- **American Elder (*Sambucus nigra* 'Variegata')** is a fast-growing shrub that reaches up to 20 feet (6 m) tall. It thrives in full sun to partial shade in moist, well-drained soil. It features dark green and cream variegated leaves and yellowish white summer blooms. It also produces black fruit in fall. It is hardy in USDA Zones 5-7.

- **Lamium (*Lamium maculatum v. album*)** is an excellent long-blooming groundcover for a dry,

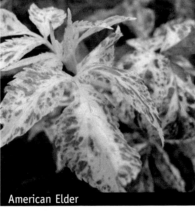
American Elder

Lamium

Pardon My Garden

The Challenge

Belinda Fairfoul and Jack Riggio had started transforming the exterior of their dream home by partially painting it and adding new windows. But the makeover magic stopped there. Beyond the porch was a weedy, wild wasteland. Belinda thought it was a problem she caught from her neighbors. Their lawn was shared with the building next door, and that yard was also neglected. She wanted to separate the spaces and have their yard stand out from others in the neighborhood. With a new baby in the family, they had planned to spend a lot of time on the porch and a nice view would be appreciated.

Jack Riggio and Belinda Fairfoul

The Goal

To tame this overrun wasteland and transform it into a tidy, colorful space distinct from other yards in the neighborhood.

The Solution

Designer Linda Parker put on her safari hat and got down to business. A quick mow of the lawn topped the priority list. Next, she needed to address the porch. The wood for the stairs was rotten. She asked carpenter Chris Pinkerton to rebuild the stairs and add a handrail on each side to define the entranceway and make it more inviting. The old paint was peeling, so it was repainted in a rust-red and golden yellow combo. She also asked Chris to build a fence along the property line to clearly divide the spaces. To complete the look, a bed of perennials was planted around the perimeter of the lawn, and hanging baskets filled with annuals were placed on the porch to dress up the space.

The 'Mow-down' on Cutting your Grass

1. Always mow your lawn when it is dry.
2. Never remove more than 1/3 of the grasses length. It will shock the root system and may take weeks to recover.
3. Mow your lawn often enough that you can leave the grass clippings where they are.
4. Vary your cutting pattern to prevent wear patterns and soil compaction.
5. Avoid mowing your lawn at midday when the sun is at its hottest.
6. Keep your mower clean and the blades sharp.

The Budget

Plant material	$ 603.00
Carpentry	$ 850.68
Furniture	$ 229.32
Paint/accessories	$ 519.34
Total	**$2202.34**

The Projects

- Repainting a wood porch
- Building a moss hanging basket

AFTER: Paint colors make this house easy to identify and make it bright and inviting. The team gave the porch some much needed T.L.C.

BEFORE (inset): Wicked and wild, this front yard scared visitors away rather than welcoming them. The overgrown yard extended from one property to the next.

The Plan

Repainting a Wood Porch

Being constantly exposed to the elements, your porch takes a beating from all the seasons. Moisture and sunlight are a good paint job's worst enemies. And the damage often shows up in the form of peeling and fading paint. Renew the look of your porch by giving it a fresh coat of paint. But don't just paint on top of of the old color. Start fresh. By taking the time to do it properly, a good paint job will allow you to enjoy the fruits of your labor for a long time.

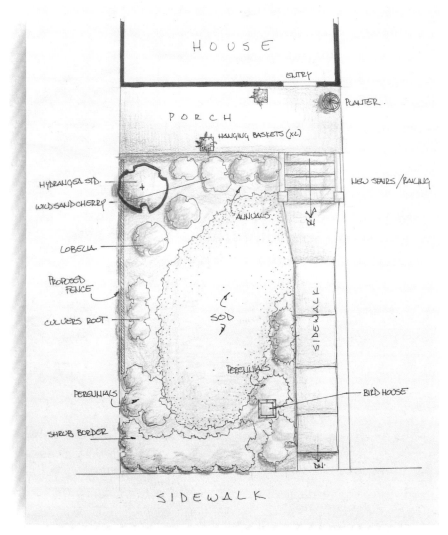

DESIGN PLAN

Labels on the design plan:

HOUSE

ENTRY

PORCH

PLANTER

HANGING BASKETS (XL)

HYDRANGEA STD.

WILD SAND CHERRY

LOBELIA

PROPOSED FENCE

CULVERS ROOT

PERENNIALS

SHRUB BORDER

ANNUALS

SOD

PERENNIALS

NEW STAIRS / RAILING

DN.

SIDEWALK

BIRD HOUSE

DN.

SIDEWALK

1. Sand the area you will be painting to loosen and remove chipped paint. Sand until smooth.

2. To decide what type of paint (latex or oil) to use, you have to determine which type was previously used. Wipe a small area with nail polish remover. If the paint comes off, it's latex-based. If it doesn't, it's oil-based. Latex can't cover oil, but oil can cover latex. If you want to cover oil with latex, apply one or more coats of special primer.

3. When primer is dry, apply colored paint. When paint is dry, apply a coat of sealant to protect the finish.

Materials you will need:

- Paint (exterior porch or floor paint is recommended; color of your choice)
- Primer (optional)
- Painter's tape (optional)
- Paint tray(s)
- Sealant
- Rollers and brushes
- Electric sander and sandpaper
- Paint scraper
- Paint rags

This porch had seen better days.

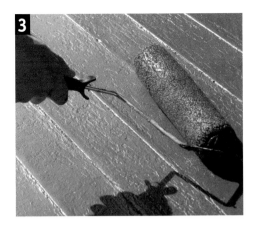

This area was cleaned and brightened up to create a welcoming entrance to the home.

Building a Moss Hanging Basket

Sphagnum moss (*Sphagnum cymbifolium*) is a perennial plant that has been used for decades as a first-aid material to dress wounds because if its excellent ability to absorb and retain moisture. The moss is composed of minute tubes similar to a sponge, which allows it to hold 20 times its weight in moisture. This characteristic has made it a popular tool for container gardening, since it prevents frequent waterings. Lining your hanging baskets with sphagnum moss is a great solution to keeping the soil moist when your water supply is limited such as on a balcony or porch.

Materials you will need:

- 1 package sphagnum moss
- Bucket
- Water, hose
- Wire hanging basket
- Cocoa liner
- Plant material (your choice)
- Potting soil (enough to fill planter)

4. Continue until you have lined the entire basket with moss.
5. Add soil and plants. Water, and hang the basket in the desired location.

1. Soak sphagnum moss in bucket filled with water according to package directions.
2. Line basket with cocoa liner.
3. When moss is thoroughly soaked, take pieces of it and stuff between the liner and wire basket pulling strands of moss through the wire for a more decorative look. Work in small sections to make the process easier.

Face Value

A home's exterior is the place of first impressions. Freshening up the exterior's appearance is something people often consider doing when they're planning on selling their property, but creating and maintaining curb appeal is worthwhile at any time. Creating curb appeal doesn't necessarily mean spending a lot of money. It's something that can be done on any budget. Here are some inexpensive ideas to spruce up your space:

■ **CLEAN UP YOUR YARD.** Rake leaves, mow the lawn, and trim the hedges. A maintained yard says oodles to visitors or potential buyers about how the interior is likely be kept up.

■ **REPAIR OR REPLACE.** Now is the time to fix shutters, a ripped screen or outdoor furniture. This goes back to the idea that a maintained exterior means a maintained interior.

■ **BRIGHTEN UP THE ENTRANCE.** Place flowers and inexpensive containers strategically to brighten up your porch and walkway.

■ **ELIMINATE CLUTTER.** Clean out any debris at the side or back of your house. This includes the garage as well.

■ **GIVE IT A NEW LOOK.** Pressure-wash or paint the exterior. If painting, coordinate colors to match the garage or shed to create a theme.

■ **ACCESSORIZE.** Add light fixtures, a mailbox, house numbers, shutters, etc., to dress up your home.

The Plants

Belinda mentioned to Linda that her yard became soaked after a heavy rain. The poor drainage was partly caused by the downspout in the garden. Linda took the moist conditions into consideration when making her plant selection. She also noted that the yard faced west, giving a mix of sun and shade.

- As the focal point in the garden, **'Tardiva' Hydrangea** (*Hydrangea paniculata* **'Tardiva'**) stood in the corner between the house and the fence, a good location to plant it on its own, as it can grow to 9 feet (2.7 m) tall and 8 feet (2.4 m) wide. A late-blooming hydrangea, its panicles of white flowers appear in August and bloom until November. The dark green foliage has a hairy texture. It thrives in partial shade and moist gardens. Hardy for USDA Zones 3-9.

Tardiva Hydrangea

- Planted by the downspout, the **Great Blue Lobelia** (*Lobelia siphilitica*) would enjoy the extra water, since it thrives in moist to wet soils and part-to-full sun conditions. It features bright blue flowers, the largest of all Lobelia species. Bloom period is July to September. It can grow to 4 feet (1.2 m) tall, making it ideal for a border plant. It's hardy for USDA Zones 3-10.

Great Blue Lobelia

- **Culver's Root** (*Veronicastrum virginicum*) is native to North America. It contains a number of chemicals that have been used in folk medicine. An elegant plant, it features white flower stalks that grow to 6 feet (1.8 m) tall. Blooming from June to August, it thrives in moist soil and full-to-partial sun. Hardy to USDA Zone 4.

Culver's Root

The Result

Success! Belinda and Jack had a great-looking front yard that was distinctly different from all the others in the neighborhood. The fence that now enclosed this space made it clear whose yard belonged to whom. And the brightly painted porch made it easy for visitors to identify. It also provided a great space to hang out and enjoy the view of the beautifully landscaped yard.

Garden in a Jiffy

The Challenge

When Anna Christensen first bought her home, her landscaping priority was to keep up with the Joneses, so she concentrated on creating curb appeal in her front yard. She knew what she wanted—a private, cozy oasis—but she didn't know how to get it. Her yard was unique and posed many challenges. It was a small, concrete parking pad enclosed by neighbours' sheds and shaded by a large oak tree. No grass, no dirt, and no problem for *The Gardening Gamble* team!

Anna Christensen and friend Peter Eno

The Goal

To turn this concrete pad into Anna's funky outdoor pad by creating an instant garden complete with lush plantings, privacy, a water feature and a seating area.

The Solution

Certified landscape designer Beth Edney knew that within the project's two-day deadline it was impossible to dig down into the concrete to build a garden, so she would have to build up instead. She designed this area with the same principles that apply to designing a balcony space; everything would have to sit at ground level. Container planting was on the project list, along with as an aboveground pond for a focal point. Colorful screens blocked the view of the sheds and provided privacy in the space. Beth also added custom hand-painted Muskoka chairs so Anna could relax and enjoy her new space.

The Projects

- Building an instant garden
- Unique copper trellis

The Budget

Plant material/soil/planters	$ 692.48
Carpentry (trellises/screens)	$ 310.08
Muskoka chairs	$ 237.98
Accessories/paint	$ 200.52
Pond/pump	$ 547.48
Total	**$1988.54**

AFTER

BEFORE

AFTER: A few plants and a pond turned this parking pad into paradise, with special seats for two.

BEFORE (inset): This concrete pad posed a challenge.

The Plan

Building an Instant Garden

You can still have an oasis in your yard even if your space lacks the traditional garden building blocks.

The key is to build everything from the ground up...literally. Here are some design elements we used that you too can incorporate into your own instant garden:

DESIGNER PLAN

■ **SCREENS OR FENCES** If you want to shield your space from prying eyes, you can plant large evergreens in big pots and line them up to create a fence. Or build some simple privacy screens and line your yard with them.

■ **PLANTS** To get a lush garden look, plant in containers—and plant lots! Customize a look by using planters of varying colors, shapes and sizes. Cluster them en masse to make it look like a garden.

■ **WATER FEATURES** What's an oasis without water? You can go with something as simple as a birdbath or as elaborate as a waterfall pond. Aboveground ponds are similar to wading pools. The pump is built in, so all you have to do is place it, fill it up, plug it in and enjoy. These ponds are also easy to store in the colder months.

■ **FURNITURE** Depending on your needs, you might want a simple bistro set for two or an elaborate eight-seat dining table. Complete your garden by adding a seating area to give you and your guests a place to sit and enjoy the view.

Unique Copper Trellis

You can spice up your everyday containers or planter boxes by adding a trellis or two. Trellises add height and structure to your garden and provide support for climbing plants. Using different materials for a trellis increases the overall impact of your container as well. Copper is one material that works well in gardens, especially as it weathers over time. This project requires intermediate skill since applying flux and soldering joints can be tricky. Always use caution arond hot objects like a propane torch.

Materials you will need:

- Four 6-foot (2 m) pieces of $^3/_4$-inch copper pipe
- Four copper T-couplings
- Four copper elbow couplings
- Flux
- Pipe cutter
- Solder
- Propane torch
- 2 feet (60 cm) 12-gauge copper wire (1 foot [30 cm] per trellis frame)

1. Measure and mark the following lengths of $^3/_4$-inch pipe:
   - two 30-inch (76.2 cm) pieces (base piece frame 1)
   - two 30 $^3/_4$-inch (78.1 cm) pieces (base piece frame 2)
   - four 18-inch (45.7 cm) pieces (upper piece)
   - four 9-inch (22.9 cm) pieces (cross piece)

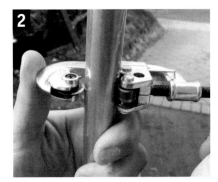

2. Use a pipe cutter to cut the pipe to make various pieces. Precut all pieces before assembly.

3. Join one 9-inch (22.9 cm) piece (cross piece) to the two 30-inch (76.2 cm) pieces (base piece) using the T-couplings to form a U shape.

4. Apply flux to joints and solder together. Always wear eye protection when using a propane torch.

5. On the other ends of the T-couplings, attach two 18-inch (45.7 cm) upper pieces to form an H shape. Apply flux and solder together.

6. Attach the elbow couplings to a 9-inch (22.9 cm) cross piece, making sure that the free ends on the couplings are facing downwards in the same direction. Attach the free ends of the couplings to the 18-inch (45.7 cm)

pieces to close off the H shape. Apply flux and solder all joints together. This completes one frame of the trellis.

Repeat steps 3-6 using the 30 $^3/_4$-inch (78.1 cm) pieces as the base to build the second frame for the trellis. Fit the cross pieces below those on the first frame to form a cross. It might be helpful to place the frames in soil so that they are firmly upright as you build the second frame.

7. When both frames are complete, wrap copper wire around the cross point at the top of the trellis. This fastens the frames together and adds a decorative touch. Push the trellis into a container of soil at least 1 foot (30 cm) deep and plant a climbing plant of your choice.

The Plants

The criteria for the plants chosen for this garden was their ability to thrive in containers and tolerance of shade, as most of the plants would be shaded by the oak tree. Since Anna's garden was shielded from some of the elements and located by the lake, the climate was unique. This allowed Beth to plant material that wouldn't normally thrive in containers.

A Garden in a Box

Container gardening is a great way for beginners to test out their green thumbs. And they're a great gardening medium for those who let their creativity flow. Just about any container can be used for planting, from purchased pots to homemade planter boxes and found objects like a boot or even a cement block. If it can hold soil, it can be a container.

Drainage is the most important thing to consider when choosing a container. Roots will not grow properly if plants are waterlogged. If your container doesn't have drainage holes, put multiple holes in the bottom. Adding some rocks will help as well.

Soil is also a key factor in successful container gardening. Ideally, your potting soil should have peat moss, vermiculite, perlite and composted manure. A good tip is to change the soil every season to ensure healthy plants.

Frequent watering is one of the drawbacks of container gardening. Due to the limited amount of water containers can hold, water evaporates quickly, so daily watering is often necessary.

A variety of plants thrive in containers. Make a bold statement in your space by using similarly colored annuals or perennials massed together. Or have your own farmer's market in your yard; many vegetables grow well in containers.

Just about any location is suitable for containers. Whether you are dressing up a patio or a balcony, a little garden in a box can have a huge impact wherever you choose to place it.

One of these plants is the **Canadian Holly (*Mahonia aquifolium*)**. It looks similar to an English Holly but it's actually a barberry shrub. It offers year-round interest: clusters of yellow flowers in spring, dark green, glossy leaflets, blue-black berries in summer and purple-bronze foliage in the fall. It's a slow-growing broadleaf evergreen, which reaches 6 feet (1.8 m) tall. Great for gardens with partial shade and ones that are wind protected. Hardy in USDA Zones 5-9.

Canadian Holly

Looking Glass Brunnera

'Looking Glass' Brunnera (*Brunnera macrophylla* 'Looking Glass') will add a touch of shimmer to your containers. It grows to about 15 feet (4.6 m) tall, and the leaves have a silver coloring, which develops by early summer. Small blue flowers bloom in spring. This perennial is shade-tolerant and requires moist soil. It also grows well as a groundcover. Little maintenance is required once established. It's very hardy and is best suited for USDA Zones 2-8.

Other plants Beth included were:

- **'Duckfoot Midnight' Coleus (*Solenostemon scutellarioides* 'Duckfoot Midnight')**

- **Lava Rose Coleus (*Coleus* 'Lava Rose')**

- **Japanese Sweet Flag (*Acorus gramineus*)**

- **Licorice Vine (*Helichrysum petiolatum*)**

Duckfoot Midnight Coleus

Lava Rose Coleus

Japanese Sweet Flag

Licorice Vine

The Result

The team overcame the problem of building on a concrete parking pad and created a cozy corner of paradise. And because all the garden elements were portable, over-wintering everything was simplified. Taking care of the plants was simple as well; all plants were easy to care for. All Anna had to do to maintain her instant garden was add water!

Surf 'n' Turf

The Challenge

Oreet Fagen and her family had been living in their home for over 20 years. A self-confessed black-thumb gardener, Oreet had done little to nothing in her backyard. Although she is an interior designer, she said she had no ideas for an outdoor space.

There was an existing deck off the main floor kitchen with a staircase leading down to the yard—an empty green rectangle. The yard had been left unfenced on the east side since Daniel was a child to allow him the freedom to play with the neighbors' children. Basically, this was a blank canvas, and the Fagens hoped *The Gardening Gamble* team could produce something extraordinary.

Oreet Fagen and son Daniel

east side, which would contain an aqua pond. In keeping with the theme, a sandy beach was a must, as well as a tiki hut beach bar for entertaining. John knew the plants must be low-maintenance so that even Oreet's black thumb could keep them growing. All in all, this landscape design was about fun and whimsy. Who says you need to travel to enjoy the tropics?

The Projects

- Building a tiki hut bar
- Constructing a pond

The Goal

To create a fun, low-maintenance theme garden, so the Fagens could entertain and enjoy their backyard beyond the deck.

The Solution

When landscape designer John Bouwmeister visited the Fagens' home he noticed the tropical beach theme in the basement. Since the basement walkout would lead directly to the garden, John decided to expand on the theme. He dubbed the look of his garden "Surf 'n' Turf". He wanted to define the yard with a partial fence on the

The Budget

Plant materials	$ 520.00
Sand, soil, rockery	$ 740.00
Carpentry (lumber for fence, tiki hut)	$ 465.00
Props, accessories	$ 355.00
TOTAL	**$2080.00**

Maintaining a Pond or Water Feature

Ponds or water features are wonderful additions to any garden. However, to fully enjoy your pond the following steps should be taken to ensure its cleanliness:

- Removal of general debris such as leaves or branches that can clog your pump.
- If you have a filter, make sure no debris is obstructing it.
- Once a year you should drain your water feature and refill with clean water. Attach a garden hose to its outlet and let it drain out, making sure not to let the pump run completely dry and burn out. Give the pump, filter and pond walls a thorough cleaning before refilling.
- You do not need to empty your pond in winter, even if you live in colder climates. However, you should remove any ice blocking the pump or water outlets.

AFTER: With a lake, beach and even a bar, there's no need to head to the cottage on weekends.

BEFORE (inset): After 20 years, the Fagens had still not done a thing with their backyard.

The Plan

Building a tiki hut bar

Any great beach needs a place a where you can sit down, relax and enjoy an ice-cold drink. Carpenter Lorne Hogan pulled out all the stops to create this beach bar.

Materials you will need:

◼ Pressure-treated lumber:
- ➤ two 4 × 4 × 12-foot posts
- ➤ two 2 × 4 × 6-foot counter-top lengths
- ➤ six 2 × 4 × 21-inch counter-top spacers
- ➤ three 2 × 4 × 7-foot roof lengths
- ➤ seven 2 × 4 × 2-foot roof spacers
- ➤ four 2 × 4 × 2-foot roof supports

- Plywood:
  - two 26-inch × 7-foot (66 cm × 2.13 m) sheets for roof
- Barnboard:
  - seven 1 × 3 ¹/₂-foot (30 cm × 1.06 m) pieces for facing under countertop
  - two 1 × 7-foot (30 cm × 2.13 m) pieces for counter-top facing
- Bamboo:
  - one 7-foot (2 m) piece for front edge of countertop
  - two 10-inch (25 cm) pieces for side edges of countertop

Other:

- Auger, shovel, or clam digger (for post holes)
- Reciprocating saw or hand saw
- Compound miter saw
- Nail gun, nails
- Screws, drill
- Stapler
- Cement
- Water
- Level
- Tar paper
- Four grass skirts (for thatching), available at party-supply stores

1. Mark out, dig, and set posts in concrete. (See "A Work of Art" on page 60 for details.) We set our posts 7 feet (2.13 m) apart.
2. Using a reciprocating or hand saw, cut out a 1 ¹/₂-foot (3.8 cm) notch into both posts for the top 2 × 4 foot brace. When the brace is inserted into the notch, you will form the complete frame.
3. Nail the countertop pieces together. When framing the countertop and roof, spacers should be set 16 inches (40.6 cm) from the center. Attach the countertop frame to the bar frame at desired height; ours was set at 3.5 feet (1.06 m). Make sure it is level so that your drinks won't slide off.
4. Miter and attach roof supports, spacers, and roof lengths according to the photo.
5. Nail both plywood pieces to roof frame. Staple tar paper onto plywood for weather-proofing.
6. Nail grass skirts to roof for authentic "tiki" look.

7. Face countertop and front of bar by nailing barnboard pieces to frame.

8. Add bamboo edge using drill and screws. Pre-drill holes to avoid splitting. Whip up a cold drink to enjoy at your new bar!

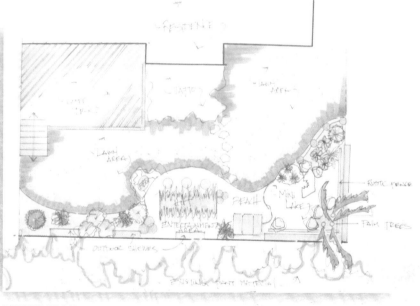

DESIGN PLAN

Constructing a Pond

Ponds are a great way to add interest to a garden and are much easier to construct than you might think. Some people worry that a pond will attract mosquitoes, but as long as you use a pump to circulate the water, you shouldn't have any problems.

Materials you will need:

- Shovel
- Landscape fabric
- Pond liner
- Stapler
- Stones
- Pump
- Water
- Aqua tablets
- Power supply

1. Dig out area for the pond to desired size and depth.

2. Cover area with landscape fabric and then cover fabric with pond liner. The fabric will prevent weed growth and puncturing of the pond liner. Your garden center can recommend the size of fabric and liner required for your desired pond size.

3. We stapled the liner to the back of the fence so that the water would look like it was disappearing behind the fence, giving the illusion of an ocean rather than a pond.

4. Place stones around outer edge of the lining to keep it in place and to disguise it.

5. Place the pump in the bottom of your pond and fill up with water, hiding the extension cord.

6. Add aqua-blue tint tablets to the water. They are safe for fish and plants and are nontoxic to humans and pets. They also help control algae.

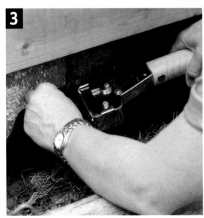

The Plants

John knew if any of the plants he incorporated into the Fagens' garden were to survive, they would have to be low-maintenance. Oreet's last venture in gardening had resulted in seven dead rose bushes, and John didn't want to see the death of any more plants. He decided to choose a variety of grasses, for their minimal maintenance needs as well as for their visual and textural enhancement of his theme.

- **Blue Lyme Grass (*Elymus arenarius*)** is a coarse-textured, blue-gray grass which thrives in full sun to light shade. It is tolerant of sand, sun and drought, and it's hardy in USDA Zones 4-9. It flowers sporadically from June to August. This fast-growing perennial can be invasive.

- **Ribbon Grass (*Phalaris arundinaceae picta*)** is a small to medium-sized ornamental grass that grows up to 3 feet (1 m) tall. It also likes full sun to partial shade and moist, well-drained soil. It is hardy in USDA Zones 4-9, and its foliage is striped green and white.

Majestic Palm

Ribbon Grass

Mountain Fire Pieris

Blue Lyme Grass

- **Mountain Fire Pieris (*Pieris japonica* 'Mountain Fire')** was chosen for its striking colors. This compact evergreen has fiery red leaves, which mature to a green color. In early spring it blooms in clusters of cascading white flowers. It thrives in sun to partial shade and is hardy in USDA Zones 5-8.

- **Majestic Palm (*Ravenia rivularis*)** was a must for the garden, because no tropical garden would be complete without a couple of palm trees. Although not terribly practical for the USDA Zone 5 climate, John knew the Fagens could enjoy their palms in the summer and bring them in as houseplants for the winter. These palms thrive in full sun to part shade, and like rich and consistently moist soil.

The Result

Two days of fun in the sun produced a tropical retreat for the Fagens. When they saw their garden, Oreet thought it was a lot of fun and Daniel was thrilled with the entertaining possibilities. The team successfully transformed a boring, blank space into a lush beach retreat that would be easy for the homeowners to maintain.

East Meets West

The Challenge

Kevin Ormsby and his friend Marsha knew what to do about interior design, but when it came to garden design, they were at a loss. Kevin's long and narrow yard was a dust bowl with a few mature trees bordering it. Entertaining was a priority for him, but his small deck made it difficult.

Kevin Ormsby (right) and friend Marsha Lederman

The Goal

To build a welcoming and functional yard that encourages Kevin to go into the garden and entertain guests.

The Solution

The mature trees in this yard inspired landscape designer Christopher Chung to create an "Asian fusion" design. Sandy soil was the base, so amending the soil to grow plants topped the list of things to do. In the hardscaping department, he planned to lay pea gravel instead of grass to keep things low-maintenance and build a stone patio that would accommodate a seating area. Large planter boxes and bamboo blinds would hide underneath the elevated deck yet still make it accessible for storage. To brighten up the space, framed painted panels would hang like simple artwork on the fence.

All in the Family

If you have a black thumb but want to try taming some houseplants, give jade (Crassula ovata) a try. It's one of the more popular houseplants because it's easy to grow. Jade is one of the approximately 300 varieties found in the genus Crassula. Native to Asia, Africa and Madagascar, plants in this genus have no typical foliage or growth characteristics. Most have thick, waxy foliage with shapes that vary from scale-like in size to several inches long. Their color varies as well, green, gray and red being the most common. As succulents, these plants thrive in dry to moist soil. While some can withstand light frost, most prefer growing in sun to semi-shade in warm climates. Crassulas come in a variety of sizes as well, from potted plants to trees. There will most likely be one to match your needs as a gardener.

The Budget

Plant material	$ 377.85
Landscape materials (stone, edging, screening)	$ 627.25
Carpentry	$ 397.64
Accessories/paint	$ 595.91
Total	**$1998.65**

The Projects

- Building a pond from a tub
- Bamboo steamer planters

AFTER

BEFORE

AFTER: Minimalist design makes a maximum impact as this yard is transformed into an Asian delight.

BEFORE (inset): Homeowner Kevin Ormsby called this dust bowl his garden.

The Plan

Building a Pond from a Tub

With a blank slate to start with, Christopher had to build the garden from scratch. By using reclaimed materials, he was able to stay on budget. He found an old bathtub and decided that it was the right size for a pond. His philosophy is anything that holds water can be an outdoor water feature.

Materials you will need:

- 1 old bathtub; cut the excess metal around the tub so that all that remains is the tub and a 3-4 inch (7.5-10 cm) lip around it (seal the drain hole, and paint the interior black.)
- Black paint and paintbrush
- Shovel
- Level
- Pond pump (optional)
- Assorted water plants
- Garden hose and water

1. Dig a hole that is wide and deep enough to accommodate the tub so that it's a snug fit. The top edge of the tub should be sitting at grade when finished.
2. Place the tub in the hole.
3. Check that it's level and make adjustments as necessary.
4. Cover the edges of the tub with soil or, as we did, with pea gravel. Fill the pond with water, add water plants and install pond pump according to package instructions.

DESIGN PLAN

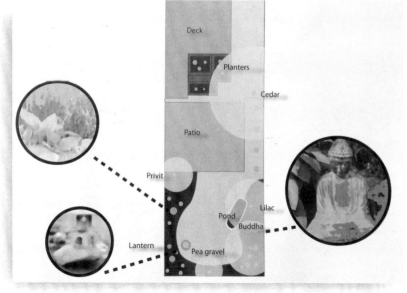

Bamboo Steamer Planters

An interesting table-setting idea is to use out-of-the-ordinary items as planters. To tie in with the "Asian fusion" theme, Christopher planted jade (*Crassula ovata*) in bamboo steamers. Steamers are shallow, making them an ideal planter for jade. This simple project made an elegant presentation.

Materials you will need:

- Bamboo steamers (your choice of size)
- Potting soil
- Small rocks
- Jade plants (keep plants to scale of steamers)—one per steamer

1. Line the bottom of the steamer with stones to allow for drainage.
2. Fill planter about half full with potting soil.
3. Place plant in steamer and fill with soil. Pack soil lightly. To ensure a healthy repotting, water lightly.

The Plants

Minimal plantings and rocks are common characteristics of Asian-inspired gardens. Christopher kept that in mind when designing this yard. He selected plants that would accent the rockery he put in place.

■ The **Japanese Painted Fern** (*Athyrium nipponicum* **'Pictum'**) is one of the more interesting ferns. This perennial showcases fronds that are metallic gray with hints of red and blue. It grows to an average of 18 inches (46 cm) tall, and the fronds grow as wide as they do tall. Great for shade gardens, this fern is hardy in USDA Zones 3-9. Its colors and texture stand out in beds and containers, and

Japanese Painted Fern

Whiteside Wood Fern

Japanese Blood Grass

Rhododendron

its creeping habit makes it a great groundcover.

■ The **Japanese Blood Grass** (*Imperata cylindrica* **'Red Baron'**) is an attractive ornamental grass with green foliage and red tips. The red color intensifies as the season progresses, and by fall, it is blood-red. This upright grass grows to 18 inches (46 cm) tall and spreads to 36 inches (91 cm). It grows best in sunny gardens; it can tolerate partial shade, but the red color will not be as vibrant. Gardens with good drainage and moist soil are perfect for this grass. Best for USDA Zones 5-9.

Japanese Rose

'Palace Passion' Heuchera

Other plants Christopher included were:

■ **Japanese Rose** (*Rosa multiflora*)

■ **Whiteside Wood Fern** (*Dryopteris dilatata* **'Crispa Whiteside'**)

■ **Rhododendron** (*Rhododendron catawbiense* **'Grandiflorum'**)

■ **Coral Bells** (*Heuchera* **'Palace Passion'**)

The Result

The yard is just what every bachelor wants—a low-maintenance garden with plenty of space to entertain. Christopher unified the space with his Asian-theme garden and created interest throughout the yard.

A Hair-Raising Gothic Garden

The Challenge

Judi Wannamaker and Jay Edwards had been in their home for just over a year. The backyard they inherited was a square patch of overgrown weeds and dirt. The idea of transforming their eyesore of a garden was too daunting, so they focused their attention on renovations indoors and ignored the outside. The space was so rundown they wouldn't even let their dog near it! They crossed their fingers and hoped *The Gardening Gamble* would help them transform what they called "the scariest garden ever seen!"

Jay Edwards and Judi Wannamaker

The Goal

To build a Gothic-theme garden, while still brightening up the space and making it a user-friendly, attractive retreat for the homeowners.

The Solution

When landscape designer Edgar Friars visited the space, his first impression was to run away screaming! The yard was dark, weedy and had extreme variances in grade; and the rickety staircase that came off the patio doors was hazardous. The frightful condition of the garden prompted Edgar to choose a Gothic theme for the garden, which he planned to enhance with accessories. He also chose to use plants with eerie and gnarled foliage to accentuate his theme.

He knew a deck was crucial to making the space functional and enjoyable. He also wanted to break up the large windowless area of the brick wall. A wall fountain covered

Gothic Roots

The Gothic period in architecture is roughly from 1200–1400 A.D. Characterized by tall buildings with pointed arches, thin walls, ribbed vaulting, columns, stained glass windows inside (to illustrate scripture) and gargoyles outside to act as protection. A 14th century plague brought poverty and an end to the Gothic era of architecture. Designer Edgar Friars uses arches, stained glass windows and a gargoyle to accentuate his Gothic theme in this garden.

in moss would create the dramatic focal point he needed to complete his design.

The Projects

- Constructing a slate wall fountain
- Ghoulish growth

The Budget

Plant materials	$ 790.00
Waterfall pump	$ 148.00
Accessories—arches, gargoyles, planters	$ 400.00
Carpentry (deck)	$ 760.00
TOTAL	**$2098.00**

AFTER

BEFORE

AFTER: Plants and accessories helped to convey Edgar's Gothic theme for the garden. A sizeable deck and a slate wall fountain were the focus of the work efforts.

BEFORE (inset): This garden was gruesome: overgrown and completely neglected. It was no wonder the homeowners were overwhelmed by the challenge of transforming this space.

The Plan

Constructing a Slate Wall Fountain

A water feature is a lovely focal point for any garden. The sight and sound of water trickling or bubbling provides a feeling of tranquility. Edgar had a huge stack of old slate tiles that he wanted to use in this garden. The patio doors were on the far right side of the house, leaving a large expanse of red brick along the left side. To detract from the brick, he decided to create a slate waterfall across this area.

We built our slate waterfall from scratch, but you could apply the following steps to any wall surface, assuming you can feed the tube from the pump to the copper pipe in behind it.

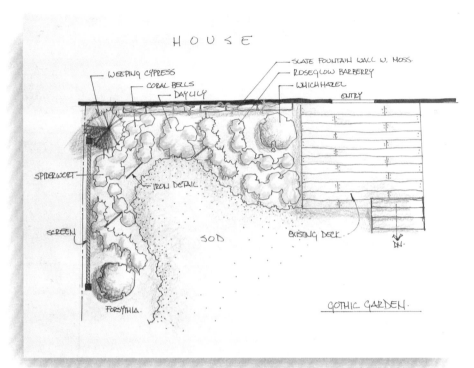

DESIGN PLAN

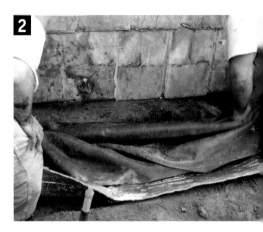

2. Insert pond liner into trench with insulation underneath. Make sure your liner is securely under or behind the wall that the water will trickle down.

3. Using a $1/16$-inch bit, drill holes in your copper pipe for the water to trickle out of. We drilled one hole every 1.5 inches (3.8 cm).

Materials you will need:

- Shovel
- Pond liner
- Sheet of silver pond insulation
- Plastic tubing (long enough to connect copper pipe and pump)
- Pond pump—large enough motor to draw the water up to the desired height.
- Copper pipe—length of water wall, ours was 8 feet (2.4 m)
- Copper T-connection

- 2 end caps for copper pipe
- Copper straps
- Drill, $1/16$-inch drill bit
- Decorative Spanish moss, optional

1. Dig a trench for your water to fall into and your pump to sit in. Your trench should be the desired length and a depth of 1.5 feet (46 cm).

TIP: Since the holes must be in a straight line, the seam on the pipe works as a useful guideline.

4. Add end caps to copper pipe. Cut pipe in half and join the T-connection between the two halves. Then attach the tubing to the T-connection on one end and the pond pump on the other. Using copper straps,

Plastic tubing

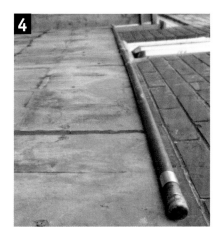

attach copper pipe to the top of wall with the holes facing down.

5. Fill trench with water and plug in pump. Add decorative Spanish moss to cover copper pipe, if desired.

Ghoulish Growth

Plants come in all shapes and sizes with interesting textures, foliage and flowers. Edgar wanted to fill his Gothic garden with some new and some older plants that were perfect for his theme.

■ The **'Young Lady' Smokebush** (*Cotinus coggygria* **'Young Lady'**) is a new smokebush that blooms vigorously, even as a young plant. It gets its name from its smoke-like blooms, but it has also been compared to a poodle. It is a hardy plant in USDA Zones 4-7 and will grow up to 6 feet (2 m) tall and wide. It thrives in full sun to partial shade and is adaptable to most soil conditions. In fall, the leaf color turns to fiery red, orange and yellow hues. Edgar felt this plant was perfect to add an eerie tone to his Gothic garden.

'Young Lady' Smokebush

■ **Witch Hazel** (*Hamamelis x intermedia* **'Arnold Promise'**) was chosen for its history as a tool for "witchers" or "diviners," who used forked branches of witch hazel wood to locate water and gold underground. In addition, witch hazel has many medicinal properties and has been used for centuries to cure

Witch Hazel

Corkscrew Hazel (with leaves)

Corkscrew Hazel (without leaves)

everything from colds to tumors.

This variety of witch hazel has interesting green leaves that turn a spectacular range of yellow, orange and red in fall. In winter, spidery yellow blooms fill the air with their sweet per-

fume. It thrives in full sun to partial shade and is hardy to USDA Zone 5.

■ **Corkscrew Hazel** (*Corylus avellana* '**Contorta**') was chosen for its twisted leaves and stems, perfect for this ghoulish garden. It is hardy to USDA Zone 4 and

thrives in full sun to part shade in well-drained soil. It has a medium growth rate, reaching heights of 10 feet (3 m). Green catkins form in early autumn and become yellow, fluffy chains in late winter.

The Magic of Mulch

Mulching is a great way to save time in your garden. Mulches keep soil moist, (which means using less water) cut down on weeds, keep plants cool, provide protection in the winter and give your beds a finished look.

Mulches come in many forms. Inorganic mulches are made of stone or plastics. Stone mulches can be attractive and do tend to stay in place, however they can migrate into the soil and complicate future digging. They also don't add organic matter to your soil, and light-colored stones can reflect heat onto surrounding plants, sometimes scorching them.

Plastic mulches or landscape fabric are effective weed barriers; however, they provide no nutritional benefits and may not be environmentally friendly.

Organic mulches are composed of plant materials such as bark, straw, leaves or grass. Over time, they decompose and add nutrients to the garden, and also promote earthworm activity. Because they decompose, you will have to replace seasonally.

We used shredded red cedar mulch in this garden. Besides looking good, cedar

mulch also smells good and its aroma helps repel insects.

Gravel

Landscape fabric

Bark mulch

Leaf mulch

Cedar mulch

Other Plants

To brighten up the dark and unappealing space, Edgar used bright plants and mulch. He wanted a variety of colored and textured foliage to offset his hair-raising garden.

- **'Amber Waves' Coral Bells** (*Heuchera x hybrida* **'Amber Waves'**) is a brand new variety of heuchera chosen for its ruffled amber-gold leaves. In full sun to partial shade, it requires moderate moisture and is hardy in USDA Zones 4-9. It is a compact low-growing perennial, with a height of 1 foot (30 cm) and a spread of 8 inches (20 cm). Pale rose-colored blooms appear in early summer.

- **'Rose Glow' Barberry** (*Berberis thunbergii* **'Rose Glow'**) is another plant with striking foliage. New leaves are rose pink, mottled with purple-red, and they mature to a deep red-purple. It likes full sun to part shade and is hardy to USDA Zone 4. This shrub will grow to 5 feet (1.5 m) tall and 4 feet (1.2 m) wide and can also be used as a hedge.

- **Forsythia** (*Forsythia* **'Fiesta'**) is an upright, mounded shrub with yellow flowers that appear in spring before its leaves do. Its leaves are variegated yellow and green and have dark red stems. It's very easy to grow, requiring full sun to light shade and well-drained soil. It grows to 3 feet (1 m) tall and 4 feet (1.2 m) wide and is hardy in USDA Zones 5-8.

Amber Waves Coral Bells

Rose Glow Barberry

Forsythia

The Result

This gruesome garden was transformed into a gorgeous, Gothic retreat. The large deck off the patio doors was a great place to sit and marvel at the garden's pièce de résistance—the slate waterfall. Edgar's reclaimed slate was a great help to his budget, and it transformed a boring brick wall into a tranquil focal point. And all of his plants were chosen for their ability to enhance the garden's Gothic theme. Stained glass windows, wire arches and a stone gargoyle were the finishing touches. Judi and Jay were thrilled with their new space and vowed not to neglect it!

Kinder-Garden

The Challenge

Derek and Deb Bell's yard was a long, narrow space bordered by neighbors and a new shed. With its limited size, they didn't know how to use the space effectively. It was often used to store their two-year-old's toys. In the small garden, they had tried planting perennials without success. Derek and Deb often entertained on their large cedar deck and wanted to look out onto a nice landscaped space. They wouldn't mind some privacy either. It was a well-maintained yard, but what it lacked was character.

Deb and Derek Bell

The Goal

To add character to a long and narrow yard by making it an über-fun playground surrounded by a blooming garden.

The Solution

Landscape designer Michael Didulka decided that since the adults had a large deck to play on, their two-year-old daughter, Katie, needed her own space. He designed a wildly colorful kid's playground for her. Most of the sod would be removed and a special hardscaping material made of rubber was installed in the shape of puzzle pieces. Some of the grass would remain, and that too would be cut into puzzle pieces. In terms of structure, two privacy screens were built at the back of the yard and a small balance beam was built for the front. Since Katie was spending most of her time here, everything was painted in bright colors. But it wasn't all for her. Michael built a cut-flower garden that blooms all season, so Mom and Dad had a view from the deck and could harvest fresh flowers for their home.

Don't eat that!

When planning a child friendly garden it is important to keep in mind that kids will often eat anything. Poisonous plants should be avoided until children are old enough to recognize and avoid them. Other plants can be harmful in the way of sharp thorns or spines, as well as skin or eye irritants. An extensive list of poisonous and irritant plants should be available through your local garden center, so do your research before you shop.

The Projects

■ Planting a cut-flower garden
■ Designing a children's garden

The Budget

Plant material	$ 674.02
Landscaping materials	$ 186.12
Custom surfacing	$ 500.00
Carpentry	$ 348.45
Paint/accessories	$ 407.39
Total	**$2115.98**

AFTER

BEFORE

AFTER: Vibrant colors make this a fun playground.

BEFORE (inset): A well-maintained yard, but it lacks character.

The Plan

A Cut-Flower Garden

Brighten up any room in your home with a bouquet of fresh flowers cut from your garden. Planting a cut-flower garden can be as simple or as complex as you'd like. Here are some tips on building your floral stock:

- Plant a selection of perennials and annuals. The perennials will guarantee your arrangements will have old standbys year after year, and the annuals will let you shake things up a bit.
- Careful planning of what you plant will ensure a lush garden all season, with blooms to spare for snipping. Choose a selection of plants that bloom at different times.
- Choose your plants based not only on color but on texture as well. Interesting foliage will liven up any arrangement.
- Keep your plant stock blooming. Feed, water and deadhead flowers regularly.

49

LANDSCAPE PLAN

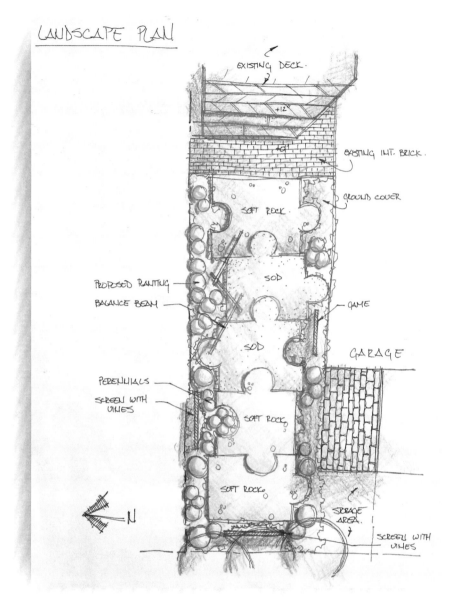

Existing deck.
+12"
Existing int. brick.
Ground cover
Soft rock.
Proposed planting
Balance beam
Game
Sod
Sod
Garage
Perennials
Screen with vines
Soft rock
Soft rock
Storage area.
N
Screen with vines

DESIGN PLAN

Blue Star Creeper (*Laurentia fluviatilis*), a colorful groundcover

A balance beam for the Bells' daughter

Toys and furniture are scaled to 'kid' size.

Designing a Children's Garden

The great outdoors is the original playground for children. Mother Nature can keep a child busy for hours with gardening, bird watching and even just playing. Getting children into the garden when they're young helps them learn to respect and appreciate the outdoors. To encourage kids to get outside, build a garden just for them using these suggested guidelines:

■ Build a safe space for them to play in. Grass, groundcovers, sand or specialty materials designed for playgrounds are great for cushioned landings. Make their area open enough so they can run and roll around freely.

■ Use bright colors in your garden to stimulate them and let them know that this space is for them to play in. Paint screens, trellises and furniture in vivid colors.

■ Scale accessories to their size. Benches, picnic tables and arbors are more fun when they're "just for me."

■ Create a play area by incorporating items that offer different activities. A wading pool, sandbox or balance beam are simple additions that can promote lots of fun. Even a semi-enclosed area can be used for hide 'n' seek or a secret garden.

Heather (*Calluna vulgaris*) attracts butterflies and bees.

■ Select plants that will attract wildlife to your garden. There are many plants that birds and butterflies flock to, and kids can learn about them in a natural classroom. Mix in a few edible plants, but be sure not to include toxic plants.

Bright and colorful—this space is designed for fun.

Create some magic in your yard by planting a butterfly garden. Butterflies are not only attractive to look at but they also pollinate wild plants and crops. The right plant material is just part of the mix when building a good garden for butterflies. They also need shelter (provided by vegetation) from the elements and a water source. But nourishment is the main reason butterflies will come to your garden. When selecting your plants, choose plants of varying heights and colors to get a variety of butterflies. Combine native and cultivated plants that will bloom at different times of the year so that there's always a food source. Here are some popular plants that are often visited by butterflies:

Butterfly Bush (*Buddleja davidii 'Pink Delight'*)
Asters (*Aster spp.*)
Sunflower (*Helianthus spp.*)

Butterfly Bush

Aster

Sunflower

The Plants

While most of the yard was devoted to being a play space, Michael did plant a beautiful cut-flower garden for Deb and Derek to enjoy. Keeping Katie in mind, he tossed in a few groundcovers to the play areas so that she would have a soft surface to play on. In his selection, he took the part-sun, part-shade space into consideration.

■ **Oriental Lily** (*Lilium* 'Stargazer') is one of the most popular oriental lilies. It has large red freckled blooms, which look great in cut flower arrangements. Very fragrant, it's a late bloomer, as flowers tend to appear mid-summer. It thrives in partial to full sun and well-drained soil. Growing to a height of 18 inches (46 cm), it's hardy for USDA Zones 3-8.

■ **Bluebeard** (*Caryopteris x clandonensis* 'Dark Knight') is also a late bloomer. Clusters of bright, blue-purple flowers appear in late summer or early fall. The blooms are set against aromatic gray-green foliage. Easy to care for, this mounded shrub grows to 3 feet (1 m) tall and wide. Ideal for full-sun gardens with well-drained soil. For continuous blooms, prune in early spring. It's hardy to USDA Zones 5-9.

■ **Delphinium** (*Delphinium* 'Summer Skies') is a hybrid plant that blooms large "candles" of light to medium blue flowers with white centers. It can bloom from early summer to frost, making it a good selection for summer interest in your garden. A tall plant, it can grow to 6 feet (2 m) in height, which may be overwhelming in smaller spaces. Grows best in partial to full sun. This perennial is hardy in USDA Zones 3-7.

Delphinium

Oriental Lily

Bluebeard

A garden of beautiful blooms

The Result

There's no question that the Bells' space had character after *The Gardening Gamble* team blew through this yard. Michael made sure there was something for everyone in the family: a fun and safe space for Katie to play in and a colorful, blooming garden for her parents to admire.

Drive-Through Garden

The Challenge

Navneet Dhaliwal thought her mom, Rani, had a pretty decent green thumb because she had landscaped the front yard all on her own. But she also thought her mom spent all of her creativity and energy out front and neglected the back. Their property size is three acres (1.2 ha), so who could blame her for putting off the work? Navneet described their space off the house as a 400-square-foot (37 m²) deck, an equal amount of interlocked brick and a whole load of grass. She said it took them close to four hours to mow the lawn. They wanted a great entertaining space that would make their friends say "wow" when they came over. Overall maintenance was a big enough chore, so they wanted a garden that was easy to care for.

Rani and Navneet Dhaliwal

The Goal

To add some function and interest to the deck area by including unique elements and plant material in the space.

The Solution

When John Bouwmeister saw the size of their yard, he knew that it would be impossible to revamp the whole space in two days, so he decided to concentrate on their existing deck area and make the biggest impact possible. The size of the space must have influenced his design; his attitude was "go big or go home!" The deck area was plain and desperately needed some character. And with so much space, installing a focal point was a given. True to his design attitude, John put an old Monte Carlo automobile in the garden as the focal point and built up a garden around it. He planted a fragrant garden among the car parts and accented it with some rockery. To add to the functionality of the space, he asked carpenter Lorne Hogan to build a raised half-hexagon deck off the existing deck so that he could make a seating area in the middle it. And to take full advantage of the size of their yard, he built a golf tee box area at the end of the garden, illuminated by the car's headlights, so that friends and family could hit balls out into the yard.

The Projects

- Softening a hardscape
- Driving the focal point home

The Budget

Plant material	$ 512.48
Rockery and soil	$ 527.87
Carpentry	$ 370.38
Furniture/accessories/paint	$ 286.40
Car	$ 150.00
Headlights and bulbs	$ 59.26
Total	**$1906.39**

AFTER

BEFORE

AFTER: An interesting focal point makes a garden unique and memorable. A new deck surrounds the prime seats for "driving" action.

BEFORE (inset): Big but boring. This place needed sprucing up.

The Plan

Softening a Hardscape

The Dhaliwals' deck was a combination of interlocking stone and resin material that ran all the way along the back of the house. John wanted to integrate the new garden into these areas of the deck but as an accent and not as its main focal point. He softened the hard edges of the interlocking brick by placing plants within the structure. This strategy breaks up the hard edges of a deck or pathway.

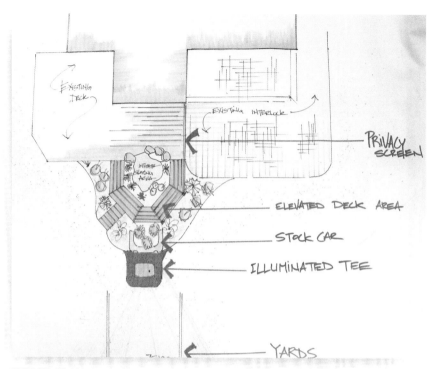

DESIGN PLAN

Labels in design plan:
EXISTING DECK
EXISTING INTERLOCK
PRIVACY SCREEN
INTIMATE EATING AREA
ELEVATED DECK AREA
STOCK CAR
ILLUMINATED TEE
YARDS

Materials you will need:

- Straight-edged shovel or crowbar
- Plant material
- Soil

1. Remove bricks using the shovel or crowbar. Dig a trench into the underlying ground material deep enough for your selected plants.
2. Backfill the trench with soil.
3. Place and plant your material.

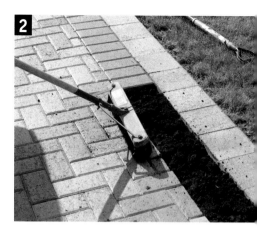

Plants can help create more interesting patio borders.

Driving the Focal Point Home

A key design principle for a well-composed garden is a focal point. Focal points help create a sense of order and anchor your garden. Many factors determine what to use for a focal point, including the size of your space, conditions of your yard, practicality of your selection and your personality. Whatever you choose, the focal point plays a major role in a well-designed space.

- **DO YOUR HOMEWORK.** Extensive planning that takes into consideration the size and conditions of your yard can help determine what you use as a focal point and where to put it. A well-planned garden incorporates the focal point into the design. Most landscape designers choose one focal point and build around it, much like John did with the car. You want to avoid making your focal point look like an afterthought or an accessory.

- **SET THE MOOD.** Look beyond traditional focal points such as statues, water features and interesting plants to create a theme or set the mood for your garden. Use your imagination, and almost anything with interesting structure, color, material or shape can be the centerpiece to your space. John chose a car because it was unique-looking and also functional, as the headlights would light up the driving range.

- **ADD A PIECE OF YOU.** A garden plan is based on personal taste, and you want to create something that includes an element that is unique and memorable. Selecting the right focal point gives you the opportunity to put a little of your personality into your garden.

- **HIGHLIGHT YOUR SELECTION.** Use pathways or walls to guide the eye to your focal point. Or place it in a sunny location so that the light hits it like a spotlight. Colorful plants around the item will draw attention and guide visitors to it.

Wild, but it works: incorporating all the elements is essential in a well-designed garden.

The Plants

With such a wide-open space and few trees close to the property, there was little shade in this yard. John considered this when he selected plants loosely based on a fragrance-theme garden. Because he was building around the car, he also selected an assortment of grasses and shrubs that were tall enough to be seen around the car.

- **St. John's Wort (*Hypericum perforatum*)** is a herb often used for treating depression. This perennial features bright yellow fragrant blooms, which appear from May to August. For the best flowering conditions, plant in full sun in well-drained soil. It grows to almost 43 inches (1.1 m) tall. Often seen in the wild, it's hardy to USDA Zone 3.

St. John's Wort

- Prized for the fragrant oil produced in the blooms, **English Lavender (*Lavandula vera*)** is a traditional plant whose scent is often found in perfumes. This shrubby plant grows to 3 feet (1 m) high and produces blue-violet flowers grown on spikes with narrow gray-green leaves. It thrives in full sun and well-drained soil. It is one of the more popular lavender varieties because of its excellent cold-hardiness. Recommended for USDA Zones 5-8.

English Lavender

- **Summersweet (*Clethra alnifolia*)** features flowers that bloom in July and emit a scent similar to that of apple pie. The flowers grow on 6-inch (15 cm) flower spikes and often last for several weeks. The entire plant grows to 6 feet (2 m) tall, making it ideal for a hedge. Prefers full to partial sun and wet soil. A great option for fall interest, it's hardy in USDA Zones 4-8.

Summersweet

- **Black-Eyed Susan (*Rudbeckia hirta*)** added some color to the garden. Blooms of yellow daisy-like flowers with a black center appear throughout the summer and fall. Deadheading is recommended to prolong blooming. It grows to 3 feet (1 m) tall in the right conditions. It's a great plant for full-to-part sun gardens with moist soil. It's hardy for USDA Zones 3–10.

Black-Eyed Susan

- **Gazania** (*Gazania rigens*) was used to soften the hardscape in the interlocking-stone area and in front of the headlights on the tee box. This was a perfect location because this annual is light-sensitive. It prefers sunny conditions—blooms open in full light and close when it's overcast or dark. Flowers can be orange, pink, red, white and yellow. It grows to 12 inches (30 cm) tall and is drought-tolerant. USDA: Perennial 8b-11.

Gazania

Work Out with Mother Nature

One of the most popular fitness activities among adults is golf. Another? Gardening, of course. Studies have shown that you can burn as many calories, if not more, because working hard in your garden can be as good for you as working out at the gym. Thirty minutes of moderate activity can decrease numerous chronic ailments such as heart disease and Type 2 diabetes. The tasks that get your heart pumping will be the most beneficial: raking, mowing the lawn, digging, etc. And don't forget that gardening is exercise, so stretch before and after your chores. Head outside to your garden for your next sweat session, and you won't even feel as if you're working out.

Activity—30 mins.	Calories burned
General gardening	162
Mowing lawn	162
Raking lawn	144
Golf, with a cart	126
Golf, carry clubs	198
Rowing machine	225
Running	400
Swimming	216
Walking	162

The Result

The Dhaliwals said they wanted a garden with "wow" factor, and John definitely delivered—big time! His driving-theme garden was a strong focal point for the deck area. And the new elevated deck allowed the garden to be viewed from another perspective. It also changed the linear shape of the space, encouraging people to step into the rest of the yard. And to top it off, the addition of the driving range turned this big, suburban yard into a fun and functional space.

A Work of Art

The Challenge

Marnie Giblin and Deland Jessop had to prioritize their renovating efforts when they bought their house—indoors or out? One look at the "before" photo tells you that work started on the inside. They bought a new shed, but lacking funds and gardening skills, they had a long way to go to build the backyard retreat they wanted. Their long and narrow yard was nothing but a dirt patch—a clean slate for *The Gardening Gamble* team.

Deland Jessop and Marnie Giblin

The Goal

To turn the ground upside down and build a unique entertaining space utilizing the entire yard.

The Solution

Designer Michael Didulka was pleased to see that he would be starting from scratch. He used the entire yard by breaking it up into two different sections, a Zen-like seating area and a traditional grassy area with a transitional bridge to connect the two. Tall privacy screens at the end of the yard would balance out the space. To finish it off, red paint on the shed and bridge brightened the space.

The Budget

Plant material	$ 268.00
Landscape materials	$ 120.00
Steel and cutting	$ 685.00
Carpentry	$ 417.00
Accessories/paint	$ 500.00
Total	**$1990.00**

The Projects

- Designing garden rooms
- Building privacy panels

For the Love of Art

Feel like your garden lacks focus? A piece of artwork might be what you need to add to get a lot of impact without a lot of work, depending on your taste. The art can be something as simple as a piece of junk found at a garage sale to something as elaborate as artist-commissioned privacy screens. Here are some tips on picking your objet d'art:

- **Consider placement.** Look for an area in your space that is lacking a focal point.
- **Consider size.** Look at how big your space is and choose something that is to scale.
- **Think outside the box.** When it comes to art, anything goes. Look for items that would never traditionally belong in a garden —metal, rubber, etc.
- **Think of the big picture.** Complement your piece with interesting and exciting colored plants. Experiment with new color and texture combinations and how they will look over time as your plants mature.

AFTER

AFTER: Art-inspired screens add privacy and a focal point to the seating area. Garden rooms (inset at left) turn the entire yard into a unique and functional space.

BEFORE (inset at right): A long, narrow yard full of dirt means a clean slate for *The Gardening Gamble* team.

BEFORE

The Plan

Designing Garden Rooms

A great design idea for a long and narrow yard is to break it up into different sections. Garden "rooms" use up much of your space and give you a chance to mix different gardening tastes. A simplified way of building garden rooms is to use plants to build your framework:

trees to create walls and ceilings, sod to create flooring and interesting plants to accessorize. If you want to take it up a notch, use hardscaping materials to add structure and texture. When designing, consider what the focal point will be in each room. Here is what Michael built for Marnie and Deland's yard:

■ SEATING AREA ROOM: Michael laid pea gravel as the flooring and built two steel privacy screens (see Design Plan p.16) for walls in this Zen-inspired room. Continuing his theme of combining steel and plant material, he accessorized the room with colored plants to brighten up and soften the coldness of the steel. He

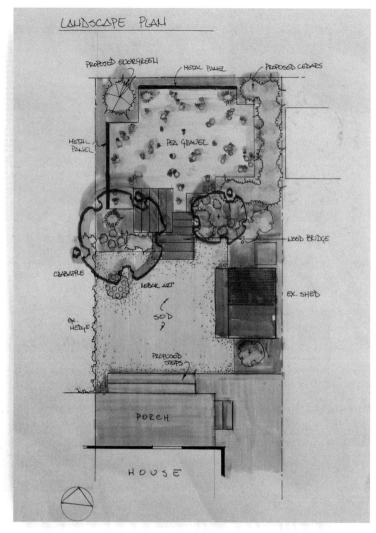

LANDSCAPE PLAN

PROPOSED EVERGREEN
METAL PANEL
PROPOSED CEDARS
METAL PANEL
PEA GRAVEL
WOOD BRIDGE
CRABAPPLE
REBAR ART
EX. SHED
EX. HEDGE
SOD
PROPOSED STEPS
PORCH
HOUSE

DESIGN PLAN

commissioned an artist to design the patterns on the steel screens, which made for a unique focal point to the mini- malist space.

- **TRADITIONAL ROOM:** Michael decided that a simple design in the other room would balance out the yard. He laid sod for a traditional look but also planted some interesting grasses and trees for height and texture. Not forgetting a focal point, Michael created "rebar art," a theme he carried over from the seating area room.

To unite the two design styles, Michael added a platform bridge that crossed over from the pea gravel to grass. He planted a 'Madonna' Crabapple tree and an Eastern Redbud along the bridge to simulate a hallway between the rooms. The red paint used on the shed and the bridge livened up the look.

Building Privacy Panels

As the main focal point of the yard, Michael wanted something unique. So he thought outside the box and came up with the concept of using steel for the privacy screens instead of traditional lattice. Regardless of the materials you choose, once you have screens, all of them are mounted the same way. These instructions are for four steel screens, which measure 4 × 8 feet (1.2 × 2.4 m). according to Michael's design, two of the screens were mounted side by side, to form one large screen. They were placed along the south and west edges of the lawn. Be sure to check local building and zoning codes before you begin.

Materials you will need:

- Six 12-foot (3.65 m) 4 × 4 posts (pressure-treated)
- Ten bags fast setting concrete
- Six sono tubes (heavy cardboard tubes for holding concrete)
- Eight $1/_4$ × 3-inch lag bolts per panel (galvanized)
- Four 4 × 8-foot (1.2 × 2.4 m) steel screens
- Auger, shovel, or clam digger
- $7/_{16}$-inch ratchet, wrench or impact driver
- $1/_4$-inch metal drill bit
- $5/_{32}$-inch wood bit
- Drill
- Measuring tape
- Level

Setting the Posts

1. Plan the site to determine where you will be setting the posts. From the first post's edge, measure 4 feet (1.2 m) to the center of the next post. Remember, two panels will be

mounted flush against each other on one post, so account for the appropriate spacing. Using the same measurement between posts, mark where the rest of the posts will go.

2. Using an auger or a shovel, dig a hole 4 feet (1.2 m) deep and 8 inches (20 cm) in diameter for each post.

3. Set a sono tube into the hole and put 2 inches (5 cm) of gravel in the bottom for drainage. Insert and center the post into the

sono tube. Using a level, check that the post is standing straight. Hold the post in place and fill the hole with dry concrete mix. The dry mix will hold the post in place after about two-thirds of the hole is filled. At this point, begin to add water to the dry concrete and mix thoroughly. Keep stirring as the remainder of the dry concrete is added. Stop a couple of inches below grade—this will let you fill the rest of the hole with soil and keep your posts tidy at the base.

4. Let the concrete cure overnight, then cut the height of the posts to suit your needs.

Mounting the Screens

1. Drill four 1-inch (2.5 cm) holes, evenly spaced, on each side of the screen, 1 inch in from the edge.
2. Align the edge of the screen to the edge of the first 4 × 4 and bolt the screen using a $1/4$ × 3-inch galvanized lag bolt for each hole. Once the post is set, it will still bend with the amount of lateral force the panels exert, so bolt one side first, level the panel and fix to the next post. When you mount the screens, the outer edges should sit flush with the post edges, and the inner edges should share the center post.
3. Use an impact gun to put the bolts in or drill a pilot hole first, and use a ratchet or wrench (a $5/32$-inch pilot hole for a 1-inch bolt).
4. Repeat to mount all the panels.

Michael and carpenter Chris secure the large metal panels.

Some Details of the Privacy-Screen Art

Plants and containers with interesting texture and shape help to soften the metal panels.

64

The Plants

Marnie and Deland's yard used to be farmland, so the nutrient-rich soil was a great foundation for the plants Michael selected. He chose a mix of plants that had different colors, textures and height.

- The **'Madonna' Crabapple** (*Malus* **'Madonna'**) is a compact, upright tree, which grows to 20 feet (6 m) tall and 10 feet (3 m) wide. It produces double white flowers in early spring and small golden-red fruit in fall. It offers interesting lush foliage, which starts out bronze and turns green at maturity. This ornamental tree is hardy to USDA Zone 5.

- **Porcupine Grass** (*Miscanthus sinensis* **'Strictus'**) is an ornamental grass. Often confused with zebra grass (*Miscanthus sinensis* 'Zebrinus'), porcupine is hardier and grows more upright. It features bright yellow variegation in horizontal bands across the leaves. It grows up to 9 feet (2.7 m) and is hardy in USDA Zones 5–10.

Other plants Michael included were:

- **Sage 'Bluebell'** (*Salvia*)
- **Day Lilies** (*Hemerocallis* **'Golden Chimes'**)
- **Eastern Redbud** (*Cercis canadensis*)
- **'Emerald' Cedar** (*Thuja occidentalis* **'Emerald'**)
- **Mock Orange 'Snowflake'** (*Philadelphus x virginalis*)
- **Corkscrew Rush Grass** (*Juncus effusus* **'Spiralis'**)
- **Purple Leaf Sandcherry** (*Prunus x cistena*)
- **Weeping Larch Tree** (*Larix decidua* **'Pendula'**)

'Madonna' crabapple

Eastern Redbud

'Emerald' Cedar

Porcupine Grass

Corkscrew Rush Grass

Weeping Larch Tree

Sage 'Bluebell'

Mock Orange 'Snowflake'

Purple Leaf Sandcherry

The Result

Escape is now a possibility for Marnie and Deland. Their unique backyard retreat gives them a place to go to when the renovation work inside becomes intolerable.

A Formal Affair

The Challenge

Debbie and Steve Bryant had been living in their home for a couple of years and had focused all their attention indoors. Their front yard was run-down and overgrown. It needed help, but they had no clue as to what to do in the garden. They decided to "bet the farm" in hopes that *The Gardening Gamble* team could pull off a winner.

The porch area was plain and needed character. The large tree in the middle of the lawn wouldn't allow the grass to grow properly, and the railway ties that shaped the garden were rotting. To top it all off, the weeds were indistinguishable from the plants.

Steve and Debbie Bryant

The Goal

To create some curb appeal for this neglected front yard with a formal parterre garden to suit the style of the Bryants' Victorian home.

The Solution

When designer Rena Hans saw the space, she knew immediately the look she wanted to create. She decided to cozy up the porch area by adding draperies for privacy and freshen it up with a coat of paint. The dead, patchy grass had to go, and she saw boxwood hedges

surrounded by shade-tolerant plants in its place. She also wanted to remove the rotting railway ties and replace them with stone retaining walls. The overgrown evergreen shrubs would also go to make way for new plantings with color and texture.

The Projects

- Constructing a retaining wall
- Planting boxwood hedges

The Budget

Plant material	$ 900.00
Retaining wall costs	$ 600.00
Accessories—table, chairs, planters, urns	$ 400.00
Paint	$ 75.00
TOTAL	**$1975.00**

AFTER

BEFORE

AFTER: Boxwood hedges and ferns were a better choice for this space. Dressings on the porch and a formal style make this home fit for a king and queen.

BEFORE (inset): This Victorian home needed a garden to suit its style.

The Plan

Constructing a Retaining Wall

A concrete-block retaining wall is an effective way to enclose a garden bed or to level a steep slope. There are many retaining-wall systems available for the do-it-yourselfer. We chose stones with a built-in interlocking lip for easy installation. You will need to plan the size and shape of your wall before determining the amount of stone you will need.

Materials you will need:

- Shovel
- Tamper
- Carpenter's level
- Limestone screenings
- Interlocking stones—the size of the stones we used was 4 × 12 × 8 $\frac{1}{2}$ inches (10 × 30 × 21.6 cm)
- Concrete adhesive
- Landscape fabric

1. Preparing the base for your retaining wall is an important step. Dig your trench 1.5 inches (3.8 cm) wider than your stones and at least 6 inches (15.25 cm) deep. Pour 4 inches (10 cm) of limestone screenings into trench. Level and tamp.

2. Lay the first course by placing each stone face down in the trench. Your base course should be buried 1 inch (2.5 cm) for each course you build. Level each stone as you go, making sure the edges touch.

3. For the second course, offset half the base of the stones, making sure the interlocking lip is facing down. Only the final course needs to be adhered with concrete adhesive.

4. Place landscape fabric behind courses to prevent weeds or soil from washing through the joints. Backfill soil against fabric to solidify the wall.

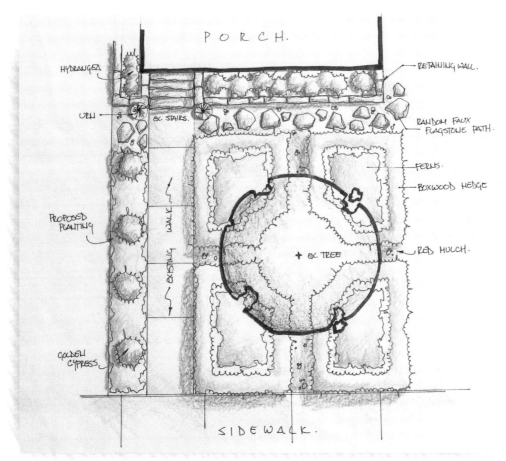

DESIGN PLAN

Planting Hedges to Create a Formal Garden

Boxwoods are an obvious choice for hedges, as they are hardy and can easily be sheared or trimmed into hedge form. Rena chose to use the **'Green Velvet' Boxwood** (*Buxus* **'Green Velvet'**). A slow grower, it will reach 3–4 feet (1–1.2 m) tall and wide. It is extremely hardy in USDA Zones 4–9. Boxwoods are traditionally planted in shady sites; however, this variety can tolerate sun as long as it receives sufficient moisture. They should be watered regularly when the top 3 inches (8 cm) of soil are dry. Boxwoods like well-drained soil.

Materials you will need:

- Shovel
- Boxwood plants
- Starter fertilizer—such as 10-52-10 or 5-15-5

1. Dig a trench (where you want your hedges to be) about 8 inches wide (20 cm) and 6–8 inches (15–20 cm) deep.
2. Lay out your boxwoods, spacing them 12–18 inches (30–46 cm) apart, to see where you should plant them.
3. Support the boxwood as you replace the soil around the roots of the plant. Push the soil firmly around the roots, ensuring that the plant is straight and at the correct soil level.

4. Water thoroughly for the first few days to settle the soil around the roots.
5. To help establish the new roots, water with water-soluble starter fertilizer.
6. Prune soon after planting, using the shortest plant as a height guideline.
7. Trim the sides of the plants as well, to encourage growth and branching in all directions.
8. Pruning can be done at any time during the active growing season, stopping six weeks before the first frost.

NOTE: the base of the hedge should be wider than the top to allow light to penetrate the lower parts of the hedge.

The Plants

The plants that Rena chose for the Bryants' front garden were all shade tolerant with interesting foliage.

■ She chose **Japanese Beech Ferns** (*Thelypteris decursive-pinnata*) for their lush, bright green foliage. The Japanese Beech Fern prefers moist or dry shade. It is hardy from USDA Zones 4 to 10 and relatively low maintenance. It has a fast growth rate and reaches heights of 1 to 2 feet (30–60 cm) tall.

- The **Korean Rock Fern** (*Polystichum tsussimense*) has dark green lacy foliage and was chosen to go with the Japanese Beech Ferns. It prefers partial shade to shade, and likes moist, well-drained soil. It is hardy from USDA Zones 5 to 9 and will grow 1 foot (30 cm) tall and wide.

- Of the 2,500 Hosta varieties on the market, Rena chose the **Robert Frost Hosta** (*Hosta* '**Robert Frost**') for its 42-inch- (107 cm) diameter clump of heart-shaped blue-green leaves with a creamy yellow margin. In late spring, the 'Robert Frost' clumps are topped with near-white flowers on 3-foot (1 m) tall scapes. All hostas are easy to grow, shade-tolerant plants. They like rich, organic soil and regular watering. Hardiness: USDA Zones 3 to 8.

Japanese Beech Ferns

Korean Rock Fern

'Robert Frost' Hosta

The Result

After two days of hard work *The Gardening Gamble* team produced a real winner! Steve and Debbie got an attractive, low-maintenance formal garden to suit their Victorian home. And, Rena successfully cleaned and cozied up the porch to create front row seats for the Bryants to enjoy their new garden.

Patio Pick-Me-Up

The Challenge

Tracy Kundell had lived in her home for just over a year. Her family loved their large swimming pool and the surrounding area, but they disliked the rest of the garden and were unsure about how to spruce it up. Tracy hated the concrete patio with its mismatched paving stones surrounded by weeds. However, she liked the yard's natural enclosure of large evergreen trees, which was great for privacy. Tracy knew the yard had the potential to be spectacular, and as an interior designer, she placed a great deal of importance on good design. But her design know-how ended as soon as she stepped outdoors. So she enlisted her friend Shannon McMahon to help her and they called on *The Gardening Gamble* to work some magic.

Tracy Kundell (right) and friend Shannon McMahon

The Goal

To revitalize an unattractive patio area and surround it with a classic flowerbed filled with plants of varying height, color and texture.

The Solution

When certified landscape designer Beth Edney visited the Kundells' home, she felt their backyard had a traditional feel to it. Tracy showed her a garden statue she'd purchased but didn't know how to incorporate into the yard. Beth had now found the inspiration for her design. She knew that entertaining was important to the Kundells and wanted to clean up the tired patio area. She imagined large garden beds surrounding the patio area, filled with evergreens and beautiful flowers. A simple yet elegant garden was the solution for this yard.

The Projects

- Staining concrete paving stones
- Constructing a concrete patio border

The Budget

Plant materials	$ 910.00
Soil, planters, willow balls (planter boxes)	$ 238.00
Carpentry	$ 860.00
Decorative stones (patio border)	$ 70.00
TOTAL	**$2078.00**

AFTER

BEFORE

AFTER: Large garden beds filled with evergreens and a new look for the patio give the space an elegant feel. Huge planter boxes filled with various colors and textures bring richness to this garden.

BEFORE (inset): This yard had a lovely pool, but the patio area was dull and tired. A concrete patio gone to the weeds and a plain stretch of sod made for a boring backyard.

The Plan

Staining Concrete Paving Stones

Replacing an old or unattractive patio is not always an option because of budgetary constraints. The good news is, however, that you can breathe new life into a tired patio with concrete stain. Beth chose to stain the Kundells' existing concrete patio, not only for budgetary reasons but also to unify the mismatched colors as.

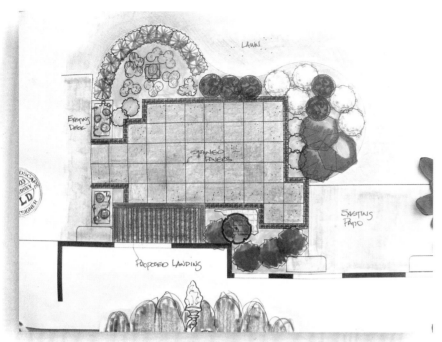

DESIGN PLAN

Materials you will need:

- Wire brush
- Paint tray
- Paintbrush, roller, staining rag
- Exterior concrete stain

1. The surface must be clean and not previously sealed before you can begin staining.
2. Apply stain with a brush, roller or staining rag. Do not thin the product.
3. Smooth stain on with long strokes in one direction.
4. Allow 24 hours to dry before applying a second coat or subjecting the surface to foot traffic. A coat of sealant for extra durability is optional.

Constructing a Concrete Patio Border

Adding an attractive border to an existing patio is another way to give it new life. It also allows you to personalize your space and have a little fun.

Materials you will need:

- Shovel (to dig out trench)
- 2 × 6 deck boards (to form the wooden frame for your border)
- $3/_4$-inch (2 cm) gravel
- $1/_2$-inch thick (1 cm) thick rebar
- Bucket/wheelbarrow (to mix concrete)
- Air-entrained concrete (concrete with air bubbles that is highly resistant to severe frost action and cycles of wetting, drying, freezing and thawing)
- Trowel (to smooth concrete)
- Decorative stones (for mosaic pattern)
- Sealer (optional)

1. Determine the width of the border you wish to create and mark accordingly.
2. Using a shovel, dig a trench for your border to a depth of 8 inches (20 cm).
3. Frame the edge of the border with wood, using 2 × 6 deck boards, which are sunk into the ground. Add 4 inches (10 cm) of $3/_4$-inch gravel along the trench. Add $1/_2$-inch thick pieces of rebar on top of the gravel. Rebar should never be less than 2 inches (5 cm) from the edge of the concrete. Pieces should overlap by a minimum of 20 bar diameters (about 10 inches [25 cm] with a $1/_2$-inch bar).

4. Mix air-entrained concrete, making sure it is not too runny, or it will spoil the mosaic design. Always use air-entrained concrete when doing a concrete project outdoors.
5. Shovel concrete into trench on top of gravel and rebar and fill to grade.

6. Smooth concrete using trowel to give a nice finish.

7. Add decorative stones to concrete to create a mosaic effect in any pattern you desire. To bring out the mosaic design, a sealant can be used once the concrete has cured (ideally, one month later).

The Plants

- Beth wanted to choose a variety of plants with different textures, colors and heights for this classic garden. For the oversized planter boxes that carpenter Chris Pinkerton built, she wanted to create something special. She started with a **Fountain Grass (*Pennisetum alopecuroides*)**, chosen for its height and texture. This was the centerpiece of her planter box. It is a fast-growing ornamental grass with densely tufted dark green leaves. In summer and autumn, it bears bristly yellow to purple cylinders. It will grow 2-4 feet (0.6-1.2 m) tall and wide. It likes full sun, regular watering and is hardy in USDA Zones 5-9.

- **Coleus 'Rustic Orange' (*Solenostemon scutellarioides*)** added instant color and texture to the planter boxes. With its burnt-orange leaves and saw-toothed gold edging, this annual plant is a wonderful addition to any group planting. There are over 60 varieties of coleus available in a wide range of colors, most reaching heights of 1.5-2 feet (46-60 cm) tall. They like moist, well-drained soil and should be well-watered but not overwatered. Many varieties like partial shade, although some, like 'Rustic Orange', have been cultivated to do well in full sun.

- In the garden beds, Beth chose **Euonymus (*Euonymus fortunei* 'Emerald 'n' Gold')** to add some interesting foliage and winter color. This fast-growing shrub thrives in full to partial sun and is tolerant of most soils. It has dark green glossy leaves with bright yellow margins that turn pinkish in winter. It will grow up to 2 feet (60 cm) tall and is hardy in USDA Zones 5-9.

Fountain Grass

Coleus 'Rustic Orange'

Euonymus

Huge planters filled with various colors and textures give this garden a richer feel.

Despite the backbreaking work involved in removing all the concrete paving stones, cleaning and staining them, then putting all of them back, the team felt it was worthwhile. The Kundells' patio was transformed from a boring and mismatched afterthought to an elegant and unified area waiting to be shown off to guests. The large planter boxes were home to a plethora of gorgeous plants with striking colors and textures. Bland and drab no more, this garden is sophisticated and chic!

Accent-uate Your Garden

From traditional bird baths and plaques to gargoyles and gnomes, garden accents are a great way to enhance your garden. They are creative focal points that express one's esthetic taste, as well as great conversation starters. Whether your tastes are traditional or a little more offbeat, there is likely a garden statue that is perfect for you. And if there isn't, well, you can create one. Dressing up your space with ornaments is a fun way to personalize it. Whether you choose items of a particular style, culture or historical period, if they mean something to you, they will add to your enjoyment of your garden.

Size is important when choosing accents for your garden. Your ornament should fit the scale of its surroundings. Make sure smaller pieces aren't lost amongst large plantings and that large items don't overshadow their areas.

In the warmer months, we spend more time outdoors than we do in, so decorating outdoor rooms is just as important as indoor ones.

Rose-Colored Garden

The Challenge

Donna Fletcher had lived in her home for a while, but the shadiness of her backyard made her anxious about trying to plant anything. A standard-sized fence enclosed the yard, with several mature trees along the perimeter adding to the garden's privacy. There was an interlocking patio on one side, which turned into a walkway wrapping around to the front of the house.

Donna's main complaints were a severe lack of sunlight and a place to relax. She wanted a peaceful spot to read and imagined a yard filled with exotic flowers and rock gardens. The foundations for a great yard were there, so all that was left for *The Gardening Gamble* team to do was to add some flavor.

Donna Fletcher and her brother Matthew Giardetti

The Goal

To add some appeal to a boring yard. Structure, rockery, pathways and plants would create a classic look in this basic garden.

The Solution

Creating some structure in this yard was a priority. Designer Rena Hans felt that the yard needed some architectural detail, and she thought a long wooden pergola off the house would work well. She would have carpenter Chris Pinkerton build a simple structure and add wrought iron inserts to jazz it up. Underneath the pergola, a stunning dining table and chairs would add to the ambience of an outdoor café.

A simple flagstone patio would become the home of a terra-cotta water feature and a large cushy chair—a perfect spot for reading.

Annual plants would be added for color in some of the beds and in hanging baskets that adorned the pergola. And, of course, no classic garden would be complete without some roses.

The Projects

- Constructing a simple flagstone patio
- Pruning roses

Caring for Outdoor Wooden Furniture

Outdoor patio furniture is an investment, so you'll want it to last as many seasons as possible. If your furniture is wooden you need to do a few things to keep it in top shape.

- Stains or scratches can be removed with a light sanding, using fine sandpaper.
- Use mild soapy water to clean furniture and rinse completely before allowing to dry in the sun.
- Use a furniture treatment oil to protect new or recently cleaned furniture. Make sure the surfaces are clean before applying oil.
- Make sure you store all wooden furniture indoors during winter (except teak or cedar).

The Budget

Plant materials	$ 500.00
Hanging baskets, water feature	$ 300.00
Accessories—furniture	$ 600.00
Carpentry (pergola, patio materials)	$ 850.00
TOTAL	**$2250.00**

AFTER

BEFORE

AFTER: A wooden pergola with iron inserts created a stunning yet simple dining area. Structure, rockery and plants created a space that made a statement. A flagstone patio and new furniture made this reading nook a peaceful retreat.

BEFORE (inset): With minimal structure, this yard was bland. It had great potential, but it needed a plan. A patch of weeds that looked forgotten, the corner of the yard had seen better days.

The Plan

Constructing a Simple Flagstone Patio

Creating a small patio area using natural flagstone doesn't have to be difficult. Donna wanted a reading area in her garden and Rena thought the corner with its dappled sunlight was the ideal spot. A loose-fitting random flagstone pattern will save you time and money, since you don't have to cut each stone to fit and don't have to use as much flagstone.

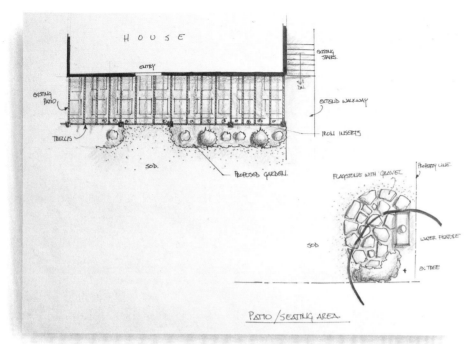

DESIGN PLAN

Materials you will need:

- Sharp-edged shovel/edger
- Hand or machine tamper
- Limestone screenings
- Flagstone
- Crushed brick
- Plastic garden edger
- Broom
- Level
- Mallet
- Rake

1. Prepare the area by removing any sod, weeds, rocks, etc.
2. Tamp ground until it is evenly packed and level.
3. Spread limestone screenings in patio area. You will need at least 2 inches (5 cm) of screenings to set the flagstones into. Tamp.
4. Lay flagstones and use a mallet to set each stone into the limestone base. We picked a random pattern. If you want the stones to be closer together, you may need to use a chisel to cut them to fit. All stones should be level with one another.
5. Disperse crushed brick between the flagstone pieces.

6. Insert plastic garden border around patio area to contain materials.
7. Sweep any excess crushed brick off of flagstones for a tidy look.

Roses Aren't Just Red

For centuries, flowers have had a language of their own. Certain flowers have always been appropriate in certain situations, and color plays an important role too. Make sure you're sending the right message with your next bouquet, especially if you're sending roses.

Color	Symbolism
Red	Love, respect
Pink	Gratitude, sympathy
White	Reverence, innocence
Yellow	Joy, friendship
Orange or Coral	Enthusiasm, desire
Lavender	Grace, gentility
Red and White	Unity
Red and Yellow	Happiness, joviality

Pruning Roses

According to designer Rena Hans, a garden just isn't a garden without roses. Along with the 'Flower Carpet' Rose, Rena also planted English hybrid roses in Donna's garden. They are crossbreeds of old roses and modern roses that are low-maintenance and highly resistant to disease and pests. However, they should be planted in groups and not placed randomly throughout the garden. They are hardy to USDA Zone 5.

Roses aren't difficult to grow, but they do have certain needs. Roses love to be fertilized. Nitrogen, phosphorus and potassium are key nutrients for strong, healthy roses. Because they are deep-rooted plants, it is more effective to water roses less often, but deeply. A 3- to 4-inch (7.5 to 10 cm) mulch base is also beneficial for keeping them hydrated and their root systems cool.

Pruning roses is another key to keeping them healthy. In warmer climates, pruning can be done in fall; otherwise, pruning is best done in early spring, as winterkill will make your efforts redundant. In very cold climates, David Austin Roses may be killed right down to the ground, but with severe pruning and fertilization, new growth should appear from below the ground.

Materials you will need:

- Pruners

1. Make sure you use clean, sharp pruners. First, cut out all diseased canes back to healthy wood. Healthy wood is the color of a green apple.
2. Make cuts at a 45-degree angle about 1 inch (2.5 cm) above an outward-facing bud.
3. Remove any stems thinner than a pencil, as they will produce only poor blooms.

Keep in mind that "housekeeping" throughout the blooming season is essential. Remove any dead leaves, fallen blooms and any other debris from your rose beds.

The Plants

Rena's plant choices were limited to shade-tolerant plants; however, she was determined to prove to Donna that despite her lack of direct sunlight, she could have an attractive garden.

Cutleaf Stephanandras

Daylily

- She chose **Cutleaf Stephanandras** (*Stephanandra incisa* **'Crispa'**) for their white spring blooms, summer green ovate leaves and autumn red-purple to red-orange foliage. They prefer partial shade or partial sun, and soil should be moist and acidic. They are hardy in USDA Zones 3-7 but need winter protection from wind. They have a fast growth rate and reach heights of 7 feet (2 m).

- **Daylily** (*Hemerocallis* **'Stella de Oro'**) has fragrant, long-blooming yellow flowers that attract butterflies and birds to the garden. It adapts well to most soil conditions and likes sun to partial shade. Hardy in USDA Zones 3-9, this perennial is a dazzling addition to any garden.

Ligularia

'Nikko Blue' Hydrangea

- **Ligularia** (*Ligularia dentata* **'Othello'**) has large greenish-purple leaves and produces stems of orange daisy flowers in late summer. It likes partial shade to shade and is hardy in USDA Zones 4-8. It requires consistent moisture and grows up to 4 feet (1.2 m) tall.

- **'Nikko Blue' Hydrangea** (*Hydrangea macrophylla* **'Nikko Blue'**) likes full shade to partial sun and is widely adaptable to many soil conditions. It has large green leaves and clusters of cream flowers that mature to a pale blue in summer. Its color is bluest if given

'Pink Flower Carpet' Rose

an acidic fertilizer. It is hardy in USDA Zones 5-9 and reaches heights of 6 feet (1.8 m) and spreads to 7 feet (2 m).

- **'Pink Flower Carpet' Rose** (*Rosa* **'Flower Carpet'**) is an extremely hardy variety of ground cover rose. They are virtually disease resistant and have a long flowering period once established. Bright pink

blooms are tinged with white, and they flower continually from spring to early winter. They tolerate almost any soil and prefer sun to partial shade.

The Result

This basic yard was transformed into a sophisticated getaway. Although the team couldn't make the sun shine into Donna's yard, they were able to make the yard more appealing. A wooden pergola with wrought-iron inserts turned a walkway into a classy sidewalk café. Perfect for dining with friends and family. The unused corner of the yard became a charming place to sit and read. And the plants gave the yard the lush color it needed. Donna was thrilled!

A Call to Order

The Challenge

Greg and Anne Shields had a massive backyard in a suburban neighborhood. It was a big enough for their kids to run around and play in. However, their kids were the only ones who used it. The yard was a mismatched combination of tastes from previous homeowners, and because the Shields didn't feel it was their own, they rarely went outside. They mostly used the space for storage. The stone patio area that was covered with a pergola was bare and boring. The house wall was covered in natural-colored lattice, and the entire area lacked a focal point. In terms of gardening, they were overwhelmed by the number of plants both in the beds that lined the patio and in those beside the stairway. The place had great potential, but the Shields needed some ideas to get started.

Greg and Anne Shields

The Goal

To unify and liven up the space, making it into an entertaining retreat à la south of France using color and various decorating elements.

The Solution

First things first: designer Rena Hans thought this space lacked personality. The basics of a great outdoor room were there; she just needed to showcase them. Her plan was to use color to unify the areas. She focused her efforts on the stone patio area off the house. The pergola would be painted and covered for a shady respite. The lattice was ripped off and the wall painted a soft yellow. And a wall-mounted water feature surrounded by a false arbor and bougainvillea created a beautiful focal point. Her accent color choices were red and orange, and they were reflected in the various accessories and furniture. Different seating areas were created throughout the space to make it functional for entertaining. The beds were cleaned up and annuals were planted for punches of color to brighten the area. A simple flagstone path was laid to encourage them to go out and enjoy the rest of the yard.

The Projects

- Building a simple flagstone pathway
- Planting amazing annuals

The Budget

Plant material	$ 520.02
Landscaping materials	$ 250.00
Carpentry	$ 222.36
Furniture	$ 680.00
Paint/accessories	$ 407.39
Total	**$2079.77**

AFTER

BEFORE

AFTER: The right colors and accessories turned this area into an entertaining retreat. A water feature and false arbor create interesting focal points on the once-blank wall.

BEFORE (inset): Mismatched. This area lacked unity and personality.

The Plan

Building a Simple Flagstone Pathway

If you're thinking about putting a pathway in your garden but don't have a lot of time or resources for an extensive job, you might want to try building a simple flagstone path. This type of path gives your yard a rustic look, and the flagstone shapes will add character.

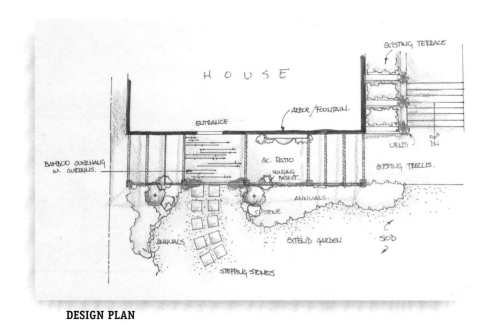

DESIGN PLAN

Materials you will need:

- Flagstones or cultured flagstone slabs (size of your choice: medium ones work best; you will need one flagstone per step on the path)
- Straight-edged shovel or edger
- Sand

1. Lay out the flagstones in the pattern of your choice. It works best if they are placed about a step apart. Using the shovel or edger, cut around the stones to make an outline of the shape.

2. Remove sod and soil beneath the stone. Dig down an inch or two deeper than the stone's thickness. Use sand as a leveling layer if needed.

3. Place the stone into the cutout and wiggle it around in the soil to settle and wedge it into the ground. The stone should be sitting at grade or just below grade to allow for easy lawn-mowing. You can jump on the stone to push it into place and compact the subgrade. Repeat steps 2-4 until path is completed.

Amazing Annuals

Annual plants are the way to go for gardeners with fickle tastes or for those who want to experiment with a style. Each season, you can change the way your garden looks by planting a new assortment. Annual plants provide instant impact with little effort. They bloom quickly and, once planted, require little maintenance beyond watering and, for some, deadheading. Their versatility almost matches the variety that's available these days:

Bougainvillea

Sunflower

Impatiens

Red impatien

Decorative clay pots of annuals

- Brightly colored annual plants are a fantastic way to brighten up a shady place. Think of yourself as an artist and the array of colorful annuals as your palette; select colors that compliment your space. Rather than spreading individual plants and colors, mass-plant one color for the most impact.
- They make excellent accessories. Annuals are a decorator's best friends. Use them as an accessory if you're dressing up a space.

Add "wow" to planters that line stairways or hanging baskets strategically placed on a porch.
- Build a cut-flower garden. Mix your selection to include annuals of different heights and complementary colors so that you can have a good assortment to choose from when making a floral arrangement.
- Annuals are great to add to your garden as a temporary fix. Use them to cover bare spots of soil.

- Hide garden eyesores with annuals. You can draw attention away from these spots by planting annuals in front of the area. Hide a composter or chainlink fence with a grouping of taller plants such as sunflowers.

What Color Is Best for Your Castle?

If you're looking to add some curb appeal or just freshen up the look of your home, consider a new coat of paint. With the value it can add to your property, a few gallons of paint can give you a lot of bang for your buck. Choosing a paint color for the exterior of your home doesn't need to be stressful. Here are some things to consider when picking a color:

- Do some research. Look through magazines and books and note what combinations appeal to you.
- Take a look around your neighborhood and see what colors the other houses on your street are painted. You don't necessarily want to be the Joneses, but

you certainly can keep up with them by choosing similar colors.
- Paint manufacturers often put together color-combination samplers. If matching colors is not your forte, then go with what the experts suggest.
- Consider how the color will look at various points in the day when sunlight is not always the strongest. Also consider how that color will look on various materials.
- When you have picked a color(s), take home a sample quart and paint a patch to see how it looks in context with the rest of the house. Decide if you can live with that color for some time.

The Plants

The Shields already had great beds of perennials. So while Rena did plant some hydrangeas to add some structure, most of the plants added to the garden were annuals. Her plant selection reflected the combination of sun and shade in the yard, but more importantly, plant choice was dependent on color. She chose plants in her accent tones for the design and strategically placed them to unite the different areas. Using large groupings, she created splashes of color that made a great impact.

- **'Non-Stop' Begonia (*Begonia tuberhybrida*)** features dramatic blooms that are at least 2 inches (5 cm) in diameter. Available in many colors, the vivid flowers bloom from mid-summer to mid-fall. It produces a mix of single (male) and double (female) blooms. Pinch single flowers to promote more double blooms. It grows best in shady spots with moist soil. Reaching up to 12 inches (30 cm) tall, it's ideal for containers or lining beds. As an added bonus, the petals are edible.

Non-Stop Begonia (female)

- **Ivy Geranium (*Pelargonium peltatum*)** is a tough and reliable plant that produces many flowers. As the name suggests, this plant is a trailing vine, and glossy leaves resemble those of ivy. The stems often grow to 3 feet (1 m). Flowers have narrow petals with less dense flower heads than the more common geranium and bloom from spring to frost. It thrives in locations with at least six hours of sun daily and requires regular watering. A fertilizer of 20-20-20 is recommended throughout the season for the best growing results. It looks great in hanging baskets and window boxes.

- **Lobelia (*Lobelia erinus*)** is a small plant, but it packs a big punch. It grows to about 10 inches (25 cm) tall and is covered with bright blue-purple flowers from spring to fall. Easy to grow, it thrives in sunny gardens with well-drained soil. It prefers the cool weather and will stop flowering when temperatures get too warm. It's available in two forms—a compact grower, which makes it ideal for mass planting, or else it has long, trailing stems, which are great for containers.

Lobelia

The Result

The team made a huge difference by working with a matching color palette. Repeating the same color accents throughout the space unified the backyard. The freshly painted wall of the house brightened up the space, and the accessories dressed it with style. The garden clean-up and new plantings of bright and colorful annuals changed the look from an overgrown jungle to an orderly garden. The result? A yard the Shields could now call their own.

Non-Stop Begonia (male)

Ivy Geranium

Training Vines

Vines can be used to add a green or flowery touch to a structure or hide unsightly items in your garden. Don't be intimidated by vines, as they are easy to grow and train. There are four basic types of vines to try in your yard.

1. **Climbing vines (*English Ivy, Climbing Hydrangea*)**
   These vines should be planted at the base of any wall or fence you wish to cover. They will send out rootlets that cling to any support they encounter and scramble upward.

2. **Tendril vines (*Grapes, Sweet Peas*)**
   Plant these vines where they can hang on to their supports. Their tendrils grow out from their stems and will wrap themselves around thin supports such as wire or other plant stems. Mature plants may require a sturdier structure to hold their weight.

3. **Twining vines (*Clematis, Mandevilla, Bougainvillea*)**
   Plant these near any trellis or arbor. As the plant grows, it will twine itself around both vertical and horizontal supports. Guide the first shoots up the structure and loosely fasten them until they establish themselves.

4. **Procumbent vines (*Jasmine, Creeping Fig*)**
   These vines crawl along the ground and must be trained to climb. Fasten them directly to a trellis or fence and secure the shoots loosely using wire or twine.

Designer Rena Hans created interest along the back wall by adding a stone fountain and a wrought iron trellis. She flanked the fountain with pots of mature Bougainvillea, and wove the climbing shrub in and out of the trellis to "train" it.

Message in a Bottle

The Challenge

In theory, new homeowner David Hughes was fairly knowledgeable about plants. However, if you looked at his yard before we got there, it was obvious that he didn't put his knowledge into practice. His yard was a large sandy pit. It did have some greenery though—in the form of weeds scattered throughout the space. But David was hoping to have a formal garden, a place he could be proud of when friends came over to dine on the deck. He cautioned that the long concrete path that ran up the center of the yard might be difficult to remove. Difficult perhaps, but not impossible. *The Gardening Gamble* team took on the job.

David Hughes (right) and friend Maher El Dahouk

The Goal

To build a beautiful garden from a large, empty space incorporating elements of a formal garden, including a central pathway, traditional plants and a unique structure.

The Solution

When certified landscape designer Beth Edney scouted this location, she was certain that a formal garden was the way to go. But she wanted to take it one step further. She divided the space in half, using the concrete pathway through the center of the yard as a guideline. And while the pathway stayed, it was softened to a mulch walkway edged with wine bottles—a quirky twist on the traditional. At the heart of it was a Beth Edney specialty, a large custom-built willow planter.

The large space needed structure, so carpenter Chris Pinkerton built a custom arbor in the back of the yard. Rustic screens created a dramatic backdrop. The beds were filled with a variety of shrubs and flowers, and sod helped complete the formal look.

The Projects

- How to lay sod
- Bottle-edging a pathway

The Budget

Plant material	$ 632.48
Landscape materials/cedar	$ 975.84
Paint and accessories	$ 128.80
Carpentry	$ 293.85
Total	**$2030.97**

AFTER

BEFORE

AFTER: A traditional garden with a modern twist. Wine-bottle edging gave this garden some personality.

BEFORE (inset): A weedy patch was what the team had to start with. This neglected garden was in dire need of help.

The Plan

How to Lay Sod

Grass is probably the most common plant you will find in any garden, and you will most certainly find it in a traditional or formal garden. But if your yard is lacking grass or your grass is lacking luster, you might want to lay some new sod. Laying sod is the quickest way to get a new lawn. The results are immediate and the steps are simple. Sod needs only 2 inches (5 cm) of soil to grow.

DESIGN PLAN

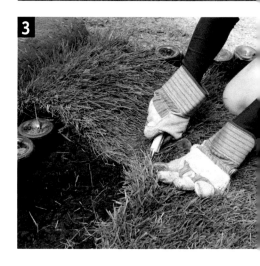

Materials you will need:

- Rolls of sod (your local garden center can help you determine the amount)
- Utility knife or sod cutter
- Drum roller
- Water, garden hose
- Rake
- Soil, peat moss (if necessary)

1. Preparation is key to a successful installation. If necessary, amend the soil and rake it free of all debris to create a smooth base. If you're starting with dry ground, moisten it in small areas at a time just before you lay the sod.

2. Line up a few rolls of sod in the area. Unroll the sod, butting the edges up tightly against one another as you unroll. This will prevent the edges from drying out. Do not overlap pieces, and stagger the seams.

3. When you get to the edge of beds or pathways, unroll enough sod to overlap the bed or path and use a utility knife to cut along the edge. At these points, cover the edges with soil to prevent them from drying out.

4. Roll over sodded area with a drum roller to smooth out bumps and help the sod make contact with the soil. Water your new lawn generously and frequently. And keep people off until you see top growth; at that point, your lawn is ready to be enjoyed!

Formal Dress Required

If your taste favors clean lines and symmetry, then a formal garden is right up your pathway. Formal gardens, often seen in public parks and gardens, are based on various European designs. Here are some common characteristics you'll find in a formal garden:

- Defined areas are the foundation of the garden. Whether through hardscaping or landscaped hedges, dividing the space into equal parts is a trademark of formal gardens.
- A pathway often leads to one or more focal points in your garden. A large planter, statue, ornamental tree or water feature are all interesting focal points.
- Choose a structure that is to scale to your space and reflects your tastes. A simple pergola, an arbor or an archway are just a few popular suggestions.
- A place to sit and take in the view is a must.
- A theme is often repeated through patterns such as mass plantings or rows of hedges. Keep in mind that overall balance is imperative to the success of formal gardens.
- Don't forget maintenance. This type of garden needs to be trimmed and tidy to look sharp.

Bottle-Edging a Pathway

Adding edging to your garden beds or pathway can improve the look of your yard. Popular materials such as railway ties and stones are great if you want a conventional look. But if you really want your space to stand out, consider edging with wine bottles. This funky look will definitely give your yard some personality. You can do this project with either a new or existing pathway/bed. If it's new, you will need to mark out the area with landscape spray so that you have a guideline.

Materials you will need:

- ■ Scraper/wire brush
- ■ Bucket
- ■ Water/dish soap
- ■ Mallet
- ■ Scrap piece of 2 × 4
- ■ Shovel (optional)
- ■ 25-oz. (750 mL) wine bottles (approx. 3 to 4 per foot [30 cm] of coverage)

1. Soak the wine bottles in soapy water and remove all labels with a scraper.
2. Using the mallet, lightly tap bottles (upside down) into the ground until the neck is buried. If you have clay-based (or other hard type) soil, use a shovel and dig a trench (approximately the same depth as the bottle-neck) that borders the pathway or garden bed.
3. Backfill soil into trench and/or between bottles to secure the bottles in place. Be sure that they are all sitting straight and at the same height. You might want to use a piece of lumber to ensure the border continues in a straight line.
4. Continue until you have completed the edging.

The Plants

Beth chose an assortment of plants that, much like the garden design, had a traditional feel. Brightly colored shrubs and flowers filled the large beds in this sunny location. The previous owners had a vegetable garden, so Beth knew that, although sandy, the soil was good. All the team did was add bags of soil to build up the beds.

- **Golden Privet (*Ligustrum x vicaryi*)** The bright golden leaves are the reason this privet is so popular. Best suited for full-sun gardens to produce intense foliage color; the leaves will turn a yellow-green color when grown in shady spots. Privet also features clusters of white blooms in spring. Its vase-like shape looks best when not pruned, and it can grow to 12 feet tall (3.65 m) and 8 feet (2.43 m) wide. It tolerates dry soil and is hardy in USDA Zones 5-8.

- **'Abbotswood' Potentilla (*Potentilla fruticosa* 'Abbotswood')** is a slow-growing mounded shrub that matures to a height and width of 3 feet (1 m). The blue-green foliage provides a great backdrop for the many large white blooms that appear from early spring to late fall. Pruning is recommended every 2-3 years to rejuvenate the plant. Adaptable to most soil types, this Potentilla is hardy from USDA Zones 2-7.

Other plants Beth included were:
- **Lobelia (*Lobelia erinus*)**
- **'Ultra Burgundy' Petunia (*Petunia integrifolia*)**
- **Weeping Pussy Willow Standard (*Salix caprea* 'Pendula')**

Golden Privet

Lobelia

'Abbotswood' Potentilla

'Ultra Burgundy' Petunia

Weeping Pussy Willow Standard

The Result

David was hoping for a formal garden when he signed up to be on the show. And he got what he wanted—sort of. Beth included many elements found in a formal garden—the willow planter focal point, an interesting structure, and a mulch pathway—but he wasn't expecting it to be lined with wine bottles. Call it formal, *Gardening Gamble* style!

95

A Tier-ful Garden

The Challenge

Jennifer and Jonathon Alton bought their home three years ago. They fell in love with the three-tiered back garden and installed a flagstone patio on the main level. That's where they ran out of creativity and know-how, so they decided to give *The Gardening Gamble* a try.

The middle tier of the garden was a slope containing a crabapple tree, some rocks and a few plants. The top level was a dirt patch, crying out for attention. And getting up to the top was a risky endeavor, via a rickety staircase and some loose rocks. They definitely needed help!

Jonathan and Jennifer Alton

360° View

When planning your garden, keep in mind what the view will be from all angles. The Altons' second-story bedroom window looks directly onto the top tier of the garden. Beth wanted to make sure she created something that was visually striking from below and straight-on so that the Altons' view would have their "room with a view."

The Goal

To make all three levels of the garden accessible and attractive.

The Solution

When certified landscape designer Beth Edney looked at the Altons' garden, she saw a real challenge. She knew that access to the middle and top tiers of the garden was crucial to its functionality. She wanted the carpenter to build a staircase and decided to make it a focal point by putting it in the center of the garden. Special plants would be used for erosion control in the mid-section, and the top tier needed colorful plants and a sitting area so that the Altons could enjoy their view.

The Projects

- Constructing a willow loveseat
- Plants for slopes and erosion control

The Budget

Plant materials	$ 900.00
Carpentry costs	$ 695.00
Pots	$ 250.00
Paint, craft supplies	$ 145.00
TOTAL	**$1990.00**

AFTER: Functionality and color were the keys to making this space a winner. A flagstone patio and willow loveseat make this area an attractive retreat.

BEFORE (inset): This three-tiered garden had great foundations but needed stairs and color. The top tier was an unused dirt patch.

The Plan

Constructing a Willow Loveseat

The top level of the garden needed a focal point and a seating area. Inspired by the woodsy feel of the area, Beth decided to build a loveseat out of bent willow that served both purposes. She wanted it to have a cozy look, so she wrapped it with rice paper, which also tied in with the color scheme.

DESIGN PLAN

Materials you will need:

- Shovel
- Willow branches—approximate lengths:
  - twelve 7-foot (2 m) pieces (outside arch)
  - eight 1 $\frac{1}{2}$-foot (45 cm) pieces (leg supports)
  - thirty 2-foot (60 cm) pieces (seat coverage)
  - eight 4 $\frac{1}{2}$-5-ft. (1.37-1.5 m) pieces (front of seat coverage)
- Pruning shears to cut willow branches to size
- Ladder
- 24–28 gauge wire
- Wirecutters
- Nail gun or hammer and nails
- Wood base for seat—we used an oak skid, plywood could also be used in a half circle shape (4 $\frac{1}{2}$-5 feet [1.37-1.5 m] wide and 1 $\frac{1}{2}$-2 feet [46 cm-60 cm] deep) with a 1 $\frac{1}{2}$-foot (46 cm) 2 × 4 nailed across the depth of the bottom as a brace
- Rice paper or ribbon—optional

1. Dig a small trench in a semi-circle shape 4 $\frac{1}{2}$-5 feet (1.37-1.5 m) wide and 1 $\frac{1}{2}$-2 feet (46-60 cm) deep. The trench should be about 6 inches (15 cm) deep.
2. Insert the 7-foot (2 m) willow branches into the trench and backfill until secure. Start with the two outside edges of semi-circle.
3. Bend the two willow branches to form an arch. Twist them together and secure with wire.
4. Repeat Steps 2 to 3 with remaining 10 branches to form the back of the loveseat, weaving them together irregularly and as tightly as desired.
5. Using a nail gun, join intersections of branches for increased stability.
6. Insert seat base using 1 $\frac{1}{2}$-foot (45 cm) willow pieces as support legs. Nail base to legs and both of them to willow arch.

7. Cover seat base with branches using nail gun. Trim branches to the same length.
8. For a cozier look, wrap outside of loveseat with a roll of Japanese rice paper, tying at the top with ribbon.

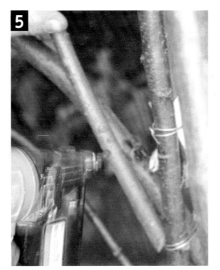

Plants for Slopes and Erosion Control

Plants can be a great way to control erosion on a slope, as their established roots help to anchor the soil.

Gardens with large sloping areas must be maintained on a regular basis to ensure that plants take hold and block out weeds. Regular maintenance includes weeding, fertilizing and replacing dead plants. Maintenance is most needed when the slope is newly planted because plants are small and weeds grow quickly in open soil. Using the right plants on slopes minimizes the effects of erosion.

When used on slopes, plants should:

- be suited to the soil, site and climate
- be perennial
- not spread rapidly outside the planted area
- require low fertilization and low maintenance

Some of the plants we chose to help with erosion control in this space:

Friend Deb Bell plants for erosion conrol on the slope.

- **Fragrant Sumac (*Rhus aromatica*)** A small, slow-growing shrub, the sumac is hardy to USDA Zone 3. It grows best in full sun to partial shade and will grow from 2-8 feet tall (0.6–2.4 m) and 5-6 feet (1.5-1.8 m) wide. It produces yellow flowers in spring and has orange-red to purple fall foliage.

- **False Spirea (*Sorbaria sorbifolia*)** This deciduous shrub is hardy to USDA Zone 2 and has a fast growth rate. It prefers full sun to part shade and moist, well-drained soil. It will grow from 5-10 feet (1.5-3 m) tall and equally wide. It produces clusters of white flowers in early summer.

- **Periwinkle (*Vinca minor*)** This evergreen groundcover is hardy from USDA Zones 3 to 8 and has a medium growth rate. It performs best in moist, well-drained soil and partial shade. It flowers blue-purple in early spring.

False Spirea

Periwinkle

Fragrant Sumac

Other Plants

Beth chose a variety of plants for the Altons' garden's needs. She wanted color, impact and texture.

- She chose to scatter pots of **'Non-Stop Rose-Pink' Begonia** (*Begonia x tuberhybrida*) and **Variegated English Ivy** (*Hedera helix* 'Variegata') around the top tier. Although both can tolerate full sun if given enough water, they also like partial shade.

- To flank the grand staircase that carpenter Chris built, Beth put two **'Oo-la-la' Bougain-villeas** (*Bougainvillea* 'Monka') in large pots for a splash of color. They are compact-growing vines, which are excellent for containers. They have magenta blooms that last longer than those of most bougainvilleas. They like full sun and, as moderate growers, require occasional pruning. In colder climates, they should be brought indoors at first frost.

- **Dark Grenadine Garden Mums** (*Chrysanthemum*) were also chosen for their striking fall color, as they bloom from September to first frost. They are hardy from USDA Zones 5-9 and prefer a sunny spot.

'Non-Stop Rose-Pink' Begonia

'Oo-la-la' Bougainvilleas

Dark Grenadine Garden Mums

The Result

After two long days of sliding up and down, the yellow team created a charming garden from Beth's design. The main attraction was the staircase, which gave the garden a grand focal point and made it user-friendly. The willow loveseat gave a natural-looking seating area where the Altons could relax and enjoy their gorgeous new garden.

All Decked Out

The Challenge

Fabian Chung bought his home and had it completely renovated. He hadn't even moved in yet when he sent a plea to *The Gardening Gamble* team to help him out. He had a large yard with a big pool and a few garden beds around the perimeter. Clueless in the garden, Fabian was also very busy and hoped for something low-maintenance. A gazebo, a waterfall and a deck to enhance the pool area were the tops of his wish list.

With a rectangular pool taking up most of the space, our team had to find a way to jazz up the perimeter, without falling in!

Fabian Chung and friend Annie Teletchea

The Goal

To create a large, round deck as a focal point and seating area on the east side of the pool, encircled by colorful flowerbeds.

The Solution

Beth Edney wanted to create an unusual deck in this space. Since the pool was the dominant feature in the garden, she wanted to enhance it and give people a place to sit and relax. She opted for a large, round deck, which hung over the pool so that those who wanted to could get their feet wet. She dressed up the deck with a stenciled leaf pattern and some cushions.

The garden beds behind the deck featured plants that wouldn't wreak havoc with the pool and also added height and color to the area. She also made mosaic stepping stones to add another special touch to the garden.

Protect Your Deck

Any wooden deck is susceptible to deterioration through sunlight, dirt, mildew and rain or snow. A wooden deck near a chlorinated pool is even more at risk. The best way to extend the life of your deck is to protect it. Whether you use paint, stain, or just leave it in its natural state, a coat of sealer or varnish will go a long way to helping protect it from the elements.

The Projects

- Creating a stencil to dress up a deck
- Making mosaic stepping stones

The Budget

Plant materials	$ 745.00
Carpentry costs (deck)	$ 992.00
Accessories—pillows, towels	$ 126.00
Craft supplies (projects)	$ 110.00
TOTAL	**$1973.00**

AFTER

BEFORE

AFTER: The round deck overhanging over the pool creates a dramatic statement in this poolside garden.

BEFORE (inset): A large pool with a perimeter of grass, this plain garden needed flowers and a great deck.

The Plan

Creating a Stencil to Dress Up a Deck

Decks come in all shapes and sizes. They can be left natural, stained, painted or dressed up according to your personal taste. Beth wanted to add a special touch to this circular deck by stenciling a leaf pattern on the longest boards. She couldn't find the stencil she wanted, so she decided to create her own. This is a great way to personalize your space with a design that you like.

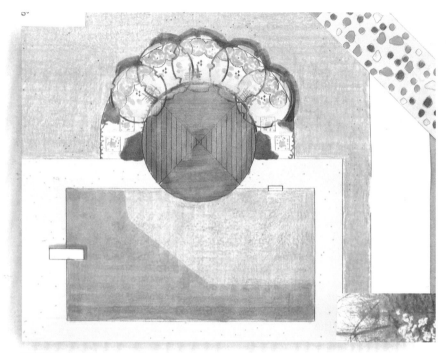

DESIGN PLAN

Materials you will need:

- Pencil
- Black marker
- A piece of paper
- A piece of acetate
- A stencil burner or utility knife
- Paint
- Sponge brush
- Fine artist's brush
- Painter's tape, low-tack or spray adhesive
- Paint
- Rags

1. Pick a design for your stencil. Using a pencil, draw the design onto a plain piece of paper. Place acetate on top of the paper. Trace the design onto the acetate with a marker. Place the acetate on a non-flammable surface and use your burner or knife to cut out the stencil design. Keep in mind that the portions you cut out will be what you see in the final design.

2. Place the stencil on the surface you wish to paint. Use painter's tape or spray adhesive to keep the stencil in place. Dip your brush into paint, wiping off any excess on a cloth so that your design does not bleed. Keep the brush as dry as possible. Gently dab brush inside the cut-out areas, working from the outside towards the center. Gently lift stencil and move to the next area, being careful not to smear the paint.

3. Let the paint dry, and then use an artist's brush to retouch any fine details as needed.

Making Mosaic Stepping Stones

Stepping stones can be the pièce de résistance of any garden. Making your own is yet another way to personalize your space. We used a simple technique to create mosaic-tile stepping stones, a project that could be applied to any surface for indoor or outdoor enjoyment.

Materials you will need:

- Stepping stones (we used ordinary concrete paving stones)
- Tiles (we used large faux-marble tiles)
- Glass pieces, in as many colors as desired
- Glass cutter
- Construction adhesive
- Grout
- Trowel, metal-toothed
- Float for grouting
- Rags
- Safety goggles

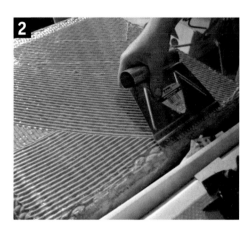

1. Apply construction adhesive to the concrete paving stone.
2. Spread adhesive on entire stone using metal-toothed trowel.
3. Lay faux-marble tile on paving stone (in the center or diagonally, as desired).

4. Arrange broken glass pieces around tile in any pattern desired. (Cut pieces to various sizes if you purchased full sheets of glass).

5. After allowing 24 hours to dry, apply grout and spread around entire paving stone, using a float.

6. Let dry and wipe off excess grout, then place in your garden and enjoy!

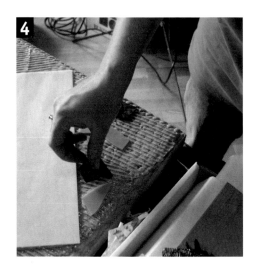

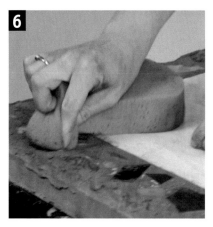

leaves that turn red-purple in fall. In early spring, it has white blooms. It is hardy in USDA Zones 5-8, and very drought- and heat-tolerant. This fast-growing tree reaches heights of up to 60 feet (18 m) and 30 feet (9 m) wide.

The Plants

All the plants for this garden were specially chosen because of their proximity to chlorinated water. They are all hardy plants that won't create a mess in the pool.

■ Designer Beth Edney wanted the garden bed to have structure and height behind the deck, so she chose five **Callery Pear** (*Pyrus calleryana* **'Chanticleer'**) trees for this purpose. It is an ornamental, narrow, thornless pear tree with glossy green

Callery Pear

'Anthony Waterer' Spirea (*Spiraea X bumulda* 'Anthony Waterer') is a low-growing shrub that does best in full to partial sun. It is hardy in USDA Zones 4-8 and has bluish-green leaves and rose-pink summer blooms. It will grow to 3 feet (1 m) tall and 5 feet (1.5 m) wide.

'Anthony Waterer' Spirea

Poolside Plants

When choosing plants for a poolside garden, keep several things in mind:

- Plants that shed, litter or have large fruit or fronds are not ideal because they will add to your pool maintenance and possibly clog your filtration system.
- Plants that attract birds and bees are also less than ideal.
- Plants with prickly or sharp thorns are best kept away from poolside gardens to avoid injuries to bathers.
- Avoid plants with unpleasant odors.
- Avoid plants that require a great deal of moisture or protection.
- Trees with deep or extensive root systems could be problematic to the pool.
- Trees such as palms and ficus are a good choice, as well as shrubs such as junipers, succulent jade plants and camellias. Perennials such as aloe, lilies, irises, yuccas, amaryllis and bird of paradise are all good poolside choices.

Coleus is a staple for landscape designers because it is low-maintenance, heat-tolerant, versatile and comes in a staggering range of colors. This annual plant does well in part sun to part shade and likes moist, well-drained soil. It grows up to 2 feet (60 cm) tall and is ideal for beds, borders and containers. Beth chose to use several varieties:

- 'Black Dragon' Coleus (*Solenostemon scutellarioides* 'Black Dragon') has deep purple and bright pink foliage.
- 'Wizard Pineapple' Coleus (*Solenostemon scutellarioides* 'Wizard Pineapple') features golden-green foliage with deep crimson edges.
- 'Wizard Velvet Red' Coleus (*Solenostemon scutellarioides* 'Wizard Velvet Red') has orange-red foliage with lime-green edges.

'Black Dragon' Coleus

'Wizard Pineapple' Coleus

'Wizard Velvet Red' Coleus

The Result

The Gardening Gamble team successfully decked out this poolside garden. A large round deck is the structural focal point for this garden, providing poolside seats for swimmers and loungers alike. The large garden bed behind the deck was filled with colorful plants and trees to give the beds some height and greenery. All Fabian had to do was dive right in!

Stone-Age Garden

The Challenge

When Lahaina and Lou Tsioutsioulas purchased their home, the enormous backyard was a major selling point. They had grand plans for an extension on the house, but the yard was so big they weren't sure what to do with it. There was an existing pond filled with koi fish, which Lou had grown very attached to; however, it was in the way of the proposed extension. He hoped for a bigger pond and an area to show off his deluxe barbecue. Lahaina simply wanted a nice space for their son to play and for entertaining.

To make an impact in this huge space, *The Gardening Gamble* team would have to concentrate their efforts in one spot. The area directly behind the house had several mature bushes and trees that offered privacy from the neighbors on the right. It was the natural choice for a great new patio!

Lahaina and Lou Tsioutsioulas

The Solution

When landscape designer Michael Didulka met with the Tsioutsioulas, he was astounded at the size of their yard. After hearing about their extension plans, he knew he wanted to build a mammoth pond to house more of Lou's beloved koi fish. He also wanted to create an interesting focal point, so he drew up plans for a large wall fountain that would spill into a 15-foot (4.6 m) pond. This would be situated at the edge of a large new patio, the perfect spot for Lou's barbecue. In order to achieve this in two days and on budget, Michael would have to recycle items found on site and use some donated materials.

The Goal

To create a spectacular al fresco dining room using natural elements such as stone, water and greenery.

The Projects

- Transplanting perennials
- Creating a simple pea gravel patio

The Budget

Plant materials	$ 145.00
Natural stone (pea gravel, patio stones)	$ 807.00
Carpentry (framing materials for wall fountain)	$ 533.00
Accessories—table, chairs, garden art	$ 496.00
TOTAL	**$1981.00**

AFTER

BEFORE

AFTER: Using stone and water, the team created a dramatic backdrop for a new patio. The wall fountain built by carpenter Lorne Hogan is a definite conversation piece!

BEFORE (inset): Perimeter plants and a blanket of sod made a large green canvas on which *The Gardening Gamble* team could work some magic.

The Plan

Transplanting Perennials

Michael wanted to create an outdoor room in the north corner of the Tsioutsioulas' garden. He decided to relocate their existing pond to make room for their future house extension. In doing so, he reused most of the existing plant material around the pond and relocated it to his new "room." "Plants are like furniture," says Michael. "When you get bored, you can move them around."

With proper care, plants can survive a move at any time; however, it is best to transplant in early spring, when the plants are dormant.

Materials you will need:

- Shovel
- Water

1. Dig the new planting hole large enough to hold the rootball.
2. Dig the plant out carefully, using the crown of the plant as a guideline for digging it out with as large a rootball as possible. This should be done quickly, with as little root exposure to air as necessary.

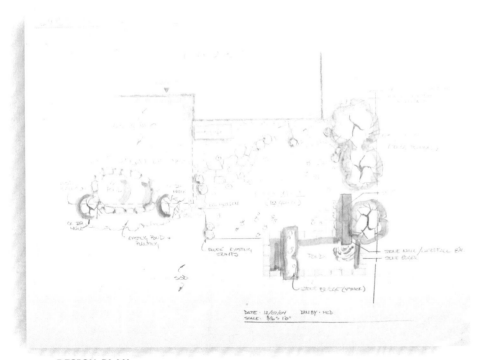

3. Place the plant in its new hole, making sure that the top of the rootball is sitting at grade, and not below, or it will suffocate. Backfill soil around the plant, making sure there are no air pockets, which may dry out the rootball.
4. Water enough to soak the ground to a depth of 1 $\frac{1}{2}$ feet (46 cm). In the coming days and weeks, water deeply, but not too frequently, to ensure the plant develops a deeper root system so it is better able to cope with stress.

DESIGN PLAN

Creating a Simple Pea-Gravel Patio

Michael wanted to create a patio area as the foundation for his outdoor room. With limited funds available, he decided to go with a pea-gravel patio, which the homeowners could upgrade in the future.

Materials you will need:

- Sod cutter or sharp-edged shovel
- Wheelbarrow
- Shovel
- Rake
- Landscape fabric
- Utility knife
- Pea gravel (enough to cover the entire surface to a depth of $1\frac{1}{2}$-2 inches (3.8-5 cm).

1. Using a sod cutter or sharp-edged shovel, lift sod from entire patio area.
2. If using a sod cutter, roll up lengths of sod for re-use elsewhere in the garden.
3. Roll out landscape fabric over area to prevent grass or weeds from growing back.
4. Use a utility knife to cut landscape fabric to size, if necessary.
5. Pour and rake pea gravel evenly over the patio area to a depth of $1\frac{1}{2}$-2 inches (3.8-5 cm).

Something Fishy

Koi are the most popular fish for use in freshwater ornamental ponds. They are a variety of the common carp and date as far back as the Chinese Western Chin Dynasty in 265 A.D. A popular hobby, watching koi swim is relaxing and watching them eat is amusing. Despite their penchant for being bottom feeders, they will eat at the surface and can even be trained to eat out of your hand.

The average koi can grow up to 3 feet (1 m) long, with growth rates of 2-4 inches (5-10 cm) per year. Healthy koi can live to more than 30 or 40 years.

When designing a koi pond, remember that bigger is better. Deeper is also better—a minimum depth of 2 feet (60 cm) is recommended. A biological filtration system is preferable to a swimming pool filter, as the latter is less effective and very costly when running 24 hours a day.

Koi are fairly resilient fish but stress can cause illness. To keep your fish happy and healthy you should:

- Feed them once a day in winter and twice a day in summer
- Keep your pond aerated and filtered 24 hours a day
- Keep their home clean, especially on the bottom
- Test your pond water every time you add fresh water
- Clean your filter twice a year
- Keep water temperature as consistent as possible
- Make sure your koi are not overcrowded: a rule of thumb is one inch (2.5 cm) of fish per ten gallons (38 L) of water.

Koi ponds are becoming a popular hobby throughout the world.

The Plants

Gardening in water is an ancient tradition dating back to Egypt in 5000 B.C. A pond is a wonderful way to add a focal point to any yard. On their own, ponds are interesting structures. Add some plants and fish, and you have created an ecosystem.

If you are unsure of which plants to select for your pond, you can always visit your local specialty garden center for advice.

Water plants are essentially divided into three groups:

1. Oxygenating plants
2. Marginal plants
3. Waterlilies and lotus

Oxygenating plants are a must, as they act as water clarifiers and help remove algae from your pond. Floating oxygenators are useful, as they provide shade for fish. Submerged oxygenators keep the water clean and pure. Place one oxygenator plant per square foot. Michael used a submerged oxygenator:, **Hornwort (*Ceratophyllum demersum*)**, in his pond. Hornworts float freely and offer shade, shelter and spawning areas for fish.

Marginal plants grow around the margin of the pond. They sit in their containers on the bottom or they can be raised up on pedestals. (Clay bricks can be stacked to create a pedestal.) Each plant has its own preferred water depth. Marginal plants also clean and shade the water. Michael used two marginal plants:

- **Horsetail** (*Equisetum sp.*)
- **Pickerel Rush** (*Pontederia cordata*)

Waterlilies and lotus provide abundant surface coverage and starve algae of the sun.

Horsetail

Pickerel Rush

The Result

A resounding success! This grassy area was converted into a large outdoor room. The dramatic stone-wall fountain feeding into a 15-foot (4.6 m) pond was the perfect backdrop for a dining area.

Michael kept his budget under control reusing a lot of existing plant material as well as various logs and stones found on-site. The cultured stone that carpenter Lorne Hogan used to face the wall fountain was kindly donated, which also helped Michael's budget immensely. All in all, this garden rocked!

The Outback

The Challenge

Nancy and Stephen Clerk are the proud owners of an 80-year-old home. They had done little to the exterior because they wanted to keep the traditional look of the home intact. However, the back porch was starting to show its age. The paint was peeling and the floor had become uneven over time. The dark beadboard ceiling and shade from the neighbor's tall cedars made the space dim and uninviting. The Clerks were fond of the area, often entertaining friends there. But they did admit that it needed an update, and they hoped *The Gardening Gamble* team could help.

Stephen and Nancy Clerk

The Goal

To give this dark porch a facelift and make it more inviting and functional for dining.

The Solution

Designer Jennifer Reynolds visited the space and saw that the back porch didn't have the charm it should have. It needed to be brightened up and made more inviting. Since the Clerks entertained a lot in this space, Jennifer's plan was to turn this porch into an outdoor dining room. Painted in shades of sand and turquoise, the space was cheered up. Painted plywood panels

Bringing the Indoors Out

A decorating trend in the last few years has been to 'bring the indoors out' and vice versa. Fabric is traditionally used indoors, however, it is making huge waves in outdoor spaces too. For years we have seen vinyl used outdoors in the way of awnings, pillows and tablecloths. Now you can find a wide variety of colors, patterns and textures in other synthetic outdoor fabrics as well.

Fabric is a great way to add privacy, to soften a hard edge or to diffuse light. Designer Jennifer Reynolds added drapery panels to the Clerk's porch to enclose the space and give it a cozy feel. If you don't want to invest in outdoor fabric or you want to change your panels seasonally, inexpensive pre-made drapery panels are an option as well.

gave the illusion of new flooring and added a decorative touch. To make it more functional for entertaining, she asked carpenter Chris Pinkerton to build a side table that attached to the porch. He also built a partial pergola, adding architectural interest, yet maintaining the traditional look of the home. A small garden bed and containers rounded out the design and the addition of coordinated accessories completed the look.

The Budget

Plant material	$ 965.22
Chandelier/accessories	$ 355.35
Containers	$ 165.49
Paint	$ 100.00
Carpentry	$ 437.81
Total	**$2023.87**

The Projects

- Get floored
- Porch pizzazz

AFTER

AFTER: A porch that's ready to welcome guests.

BEFORE (inset): This porch is plain and dark. It needed updating.

BEFORE

The Plan

Get Floored

Replacing the flooring on your porch or deck can be a costly and time-consuming venture. Another option you may want to consider is covering the floor with plywood. This is a quick and cost-effective cosmetic fix that gives the illusion of a new floor.

Jennifer painted a decorative diamond pattern on the plywood so that it would look like a rug. This had a huge impact in the transformation. Designs and color schemes can be as simple or elaborate as desired.

FRENCH DOORS

PROPOSED LEDGE + OVERHANG

PORCH

DETAILED SIDE PANEL

STAIRS

EX. PLANT MATERIAL.

DN.

* PROPOSED PLANTING

* • PEEGEE HYDRANGEA.
  • BLUE JUNIPER
  • GRASSES
  • CARPET ROSES
  • HOSTA
  • RUDBECKIA
  • ASTERS
  • BUTTERFLY BUSH
  • BLUE MIST SPIREA

SOD

SOD

EXTEND PATHWAY TO MEET STAIRS.

DN.

DESIGN PLAN

Materials you will need:

- Sheets of plywood (size determined by the area size you are recovering)
- Circular saw
- Measuring tape
- Pencil
- Paint (your color preference)
- Sealant (optional)
- Primer
- Rollers and brushes
- Paint tray(s)
- Painter's tape
- Exterior construction adhesive
- Nails
- Hammer

1. Measure and precut plywood to fit the floor. Building this project in panels makes it easier to fit. Prime all pieces on both sides.

2. When surface is dry, tape off the pattern you want to create. Remember to lay pieces together in the order you will put them on the floor.

3. Paint your pattern. You might want to paint a couple of coats to ensure good coverage.

4. When dry, remove painter's tape. If it's a high-traffic area, you may want to apply a sealant.

5. On the porch, apply a layer of exterior construction adhesive.
6. Working one panel at a time, lay the pieces in place keeping the design in mind. When all panels are in place, walk on top to ensure they adhere to the original flooring. Finish by nailing the panels to keep them in place.

Colormania

Color makes a huge impact in a yard. From plant material to accessories, consider what kind of atmosphere you want to create. When planning your outdoor space, choose your colors carefully, as some schemes are better suited to particular spaces.

Small spaces:
Colors such as blue and green are restful and work best in smaller gardens. Keep it simple; use only one or two shades.

Large spaces:
Active colors such as reds, oranges and yellows are perfect choices for focal points in larger gardens. Since people are drawn to bright colors, they will want to get up close to admire your handiwork. These bold colors also make a big visual impact when planted en masse.

Sunny spaces:
When choosing colors for your furniture, avoid dark colors, as they absorb heat and make for uncomfortable seating. Neutrals are your best bet, but avoid white. The reflection will create undesirable glare.

Shady spaces:
Light, white or bright furniture and accessories work best to brighten up a space.

Porch Pizzazz

More and more people are spending their time outdoors, whether relaxing, entertaining or dining. So it's no surprise that you want your outdoor space to look stylish and be comfortable. After all, your yard is an extension of your home. A great design tip is to think of the yard as another room in your home. And don't forget the porch. A porch—in the front or back—gives a preview of what your guests can find inside. It needs to be bright and welcoming like a gateway into your home. Punch up your porch and give it some pizzazz. Here's how:

- Give your porch a fresh coat of paint. Choose colors that compliment your home but also have impact. If you're worried about going all the way with one color you like, try it as an accent color.
- Start from the ground up. Paint an interesting pattern on the floor, or paint and seal heavy canvas to use as an outdoor rug. Also, upgrade the traditional porch light. Use chandeliers or other interesting light fixtures outside. Many stores now carry interesting fixtures specifically for outdoor use.
- Invest in good furniture. Outdoor furniture has come a long way since the days of resin. The styles and fabrics can be stylish and modern. Manufacturers are now coming out with lines that look like they should be indoors but are built to withstand the elements. You can definitely find something that matches your design taste.
- Decorate! Get past traditional window boxes and decorate your porch with interesting and colorful containers; use interesting baskets or buckets to plant your floral favorites. Hang a mirror on the wall or try mirror tiles on the ceiling to open up the space. Use curtains to soften a look and create some privacy.

The Plants

Mature trees dappled the Clerks' yard with sunshine, so Jennifer had to choose plants that would tolerate a partly sunny yard. She chose some standards for the garden around the porch: a hydrangea as the focal point and some boxwoods to border the bed. But the majority of her plants were theme-based. She wanted to create a relaxing atmosphere, so she chose plants that were shades of blue. Most of them were planted in containers, which gave her the flexibility to place them in ideal positions.

Blue Star Flower

Icicle Pansy 'Sapphire Splash'

- **Blue Star Flower (*Amsonia*)**
  This hardy perennial offers clusters of dainty blue flowers and interesting foliage that turns yellow-gold in fall. It grows to 50 inches (1.27 m) tall and 60 inches (1.5 m) wide. Great for moist-soil gardens with part shade to full sun. A low-maintenance plant, it's hardy to USDA Zones 5-9.

- **Golden Blue Mist Spirea (*Caryopteris incana* 'Jason')** is a flowering shrub originally from Eastern Asia. It features bright yellow foliage and amethyst-blue flowers. It's a late bloomer so the flowers appear in summer and carry on into the fall. It grows the size of a small shrub, 3 feet (1 m) tall and wide. It thrives in full sun gardens with well-drained soil. Hardy to USDA Zones 5-9.

Golden Blue Mist

- **Icicle Pansy 'Sapphire Splash' (*Viola hiemalis*)** is a cold-hardy annual and tends to bloom until frost. The key is to plant them late in the summer or in early fall. The blooms are small but intense in color. They grow to 12 inches (30 cm) in height and need to be spaced 8 inches (20 cm) apart to grow when planted. They thrive in full to partial sun and look great mixed in with other plants.

The Result

The Clerks' new porch was a welcome sight. It radiated charm and elegance and became the perfect place for entertaining friends. Brightened up with the paint, mirror and plants, the porch invited visitors to the home. Chris's side table was a handy addition, as it gave the homeowners more room to work at mealtimes. All in all, the team turned the porch into a functional space with flair!

119

A Garden that Soars to New Heights

The Challenge

Actors Camilla Scott and Paul Eves have played all kinds of roles in their careers. However, the one role they wanted to perfect was that of gardener. They recently moved into a condo, and the balcony space was builder basic. The size was reasonable, 200 square feet (18.6 m²), but asking them to design it was not. This couple wanted a chic space to entertain friends and have some green space in a concrete jungle. Enter stage left—*The Gardening Gamble* team.

Paul Eves and Camilla Scott

The Goal

To take gardening to a new level and have several elements of a traditional backyard fit into a balcony space seven stories up.

The Solution

Designer Rena Hans was going for an urban feel with a touch of the exotic when she planned this balcony. She decided that entertaining was going to be the main function of the area, so a chic seating area featuring a stainless steel table would be the focal point of her design. A custom planter box and a tribal-style bench would balance the balcony on each end. And to make it really feel like a backyard, deck tiles would be laid on the cement floor to mimic a back deck. Accent plants and trendy accessories would tie the whole look together.

Take-away Gardens

If you reside in an apartment building or condominium, chances are you may not reside there for many years to come. Just because your living arrangements aren't permanent doesn't mean you can't put down some roots. It's easy enough to make your garden transportable to another balcony, or a backyard space. When planning an impermanent garden make sure to avoid wall fixtures and ensure trellises are removable. Buying lightweight planter boxes and containers will also help you when moving day rolls around.

The Projects

- Antiquing furniture
- Customizing planter boxes

The Budget

Plant material	$ 350.00
Furniture/accessories	$ 450.00
Deck tiles	$ 480.00
Stainless steel table	$ 600.00
Carpentry	$ 219.99
Total	**$2099.99**

AFTER: Attractive plants and chic furniture made this space one to 'dine' for.

BEFORE (inset): Rena saw the potential of this bare balcony.

The Plan

Antiquing Furniture

Weathered furniture is all the rage, but you don't have to shell out the big bucks at the local antique store to get this look in your yard. This design job is a simple afternoon project, but the result will look like it took years to accomplish.

Materials you will need:

- Latex or oil-based paint (You will need to choose two colors— a base color and a darker color that will pick up the grain of the wood. There is no science to this, just pick colors you like.)
- Paint rollers
- Small paintbrush
- Paint trays
- Old rags

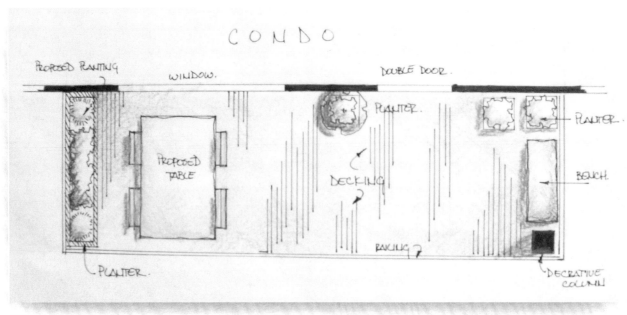

CONDO

PROPOSED PLANTING
WINDOW.
DOUBLE DOOR.
PLANTER.
PLANTER.
PROPOSED TABLE
DECKING
BENCH.
RAILING
PLANTER.
DECORATIVE COLUMN

DESIGN PLAN

1. Roll or brush (the photo has a brush) your base color onto the chair. Coverage should be even, but it doesn't have to be perfect.

2. Once the base coat has dried thoroughly, take your second color and dip your brush into the can.

3. Then tap the brush lightly on a rag to remove most of the paint.

4. Working in small sections, paint the color on using light, random strokes. You want the paint to create fine lines and streaks, much like a wood grain. Never let a section dry before starting the next.

TIP: A light sanding of areas that would get the most wear and tear will further add to the distressed and aged look of the piece.

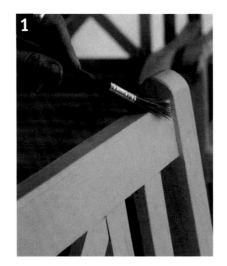

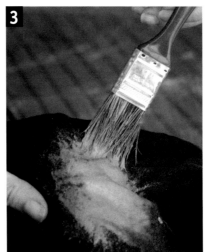

A classy table and chairs added elegance to this small space.

1. Mark and cut the 2 × 3s into the following pieces of wood:
   ➤ four 12 inches long (30 cm)
   ➤ two 14 inches long (35 cm)
2. Build a square using the four shorter pieces and screw together.
3. Measure and mark the center point of the ends of the longer pieces. Using a compound miter saw, miter the ends to a point.
4. Insert one piece into the square diagonally. Lay the second one across it to make an X. Mark the cross points.
5. Cut the second longer piece at the cross-point markings.

Customizing Planter Boxes

A planter box on a balcony is a great way to unite your plants and have them growing in one container as they would in a garden bed. Not only can you customize the size of the planter box to fit your space, you can dress up your planter box to add another dimension to your design. Whether you use paint or trim, you can take your planter boxes from ordinary to extraordinary. These instructions are to add a protruding design to a planter.

Materials you will need:

- one plain wooden planter, 7 × 24 × 18 inches (18 × 60 × 45 cm)
- three untreated 2 × 3s, 8 feet (2.4 m) in length
- 3-inch screws (approx. 30)
- Drill
- Carpenter's square
- Compound miter saw
- Router
- Pencil
- Hammer
- Paint and paintbrush

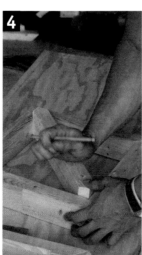

6. Place the two halves in the square to complete the X. If necessary, tap them in lightly with a hammer.
7. Use a router to bevel the front edges of the square.
8. Repeat steps 1-7 to make two more squares. Space the squares evenly along the front of the planter and screw them into place. Paint the planter.

The Plants

Balcony spaces tend to have their own climate zone. Rena selected plants that would thrive in containers, and survive the extra exposure to the sun and wind. She chose a colorful combination of annuals and perennials to brighten up the space and even threw some tall grasses into the mix to create some privacy from the neighbors.

- **Flowering Kale (*Brassica oleracea*)** was one of her choices. This ornamental annual has showy foliage with a mix of colors, including purple, pink and cream, a great early-fall addition to your garden. Colors tend to intensify at the first light frost. It grows to 18 inches (45 cm) high and 12 inches (30 cm) wide. Flowering Kale thrives in full sun and moist, well-drained soil. The leaves can be eaten as well as admired.

- **Florist Chrysanthemum (*Dendranthema x grandiflorum*)** is a perennial that grows well both in containers and in the ground. It features decorative blooms that come in almost all colors except blue and red. Some types grow as high as 3 feet (1 cm) and most are adaptable to a variety of soil types. It thrives in full sun, and while some may be described as winter-hardy, most are not. Chrysanthemums grow best in USDA Zones 4-7.

Other plants Rena included were:

- **Purple Fountain Grass (*Pennisetum alopecuroides setaceum* 'Rubrum')**
- **'Pink Diamond' Hydrangea (*Hydrangea paniculata* 'Pink Diamond')**
- **Peace Lily (*Spathiphyllum clevelandii*)**

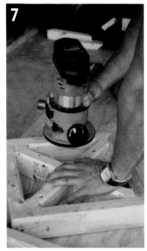

Flowering Kale

Florist Chrysanthemum

Purple Fountain Grass

'Pink Diamond' Hydrangea

Designing for Balconies

200 square feet may sound small, but with the right design, the impact your balcony makes could be big. Here are some basics:

- Check with a professional on the structure of your space. Most balconies can't withstand the weight of items you may want to incorporate. Think of lightweight alternatives to your favorites.
- Decide how you are going to use the space. Entertaining, eating, storage? Make that the focal point of your balcony.
- When will you use the space? Seasonally? Even if you're only out there for part of the year, you'll want to have interest all year long.
- If you're going to have plants, select ones that are container-friendly. Perennials may be the way to go if you're a low-maintenance kind of gardener. Also consider climate.

- Balconies have their own climate zone because of unique exposure to the sun and wind. Select plants that are one full zone hardier than what you would select for a garden at ground level. Make sure you have an adequate water supply for your garden. Overhangs will likely prevent your plants from getting rainfall.
- Style is critical to a balcony garden. Treat the space as another room in your home and decorate it as you have indoors. Stylish outdoor furniture is widely available. Look past the traditional plastic furniture though. You need to have furniture that won't blow away on windy days.

For such a small space, there is a lot to consider. But when your guests are raving about how your place looks, relish knowing that every inch of it is yours.

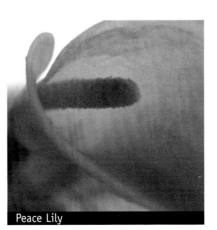
Peace Lily

The Result

Rena turned this blah balcony into a funky, functional space for Camilla and Paul. They now have a small backyard for their condo, deck included! Urban-chic furniture and interesting plants create a stylish backdrop for their dinner parties.

DISHing the Dirt

The Challenge

Nathalie Malette had been living in her home for six years. She inherited a large deck that she enjoyed sitting on despite its shady location. The rest of the long, rectangular yard contained grass, which was where her two kids played. A small shed sat opposite the deck, and toys and bikes were scattered around the perimeter. This yard lacked imagination and plants. Nathalie wanted space for her kids to play, but she also wanted to entertain in her sunny yard. She loved the *chiminea* on her deck and hoped it could become a focal point elsewhere in the garden.

Nathalie Malette (right) and friend Christine Palmer

The Goal

To clean up the space and create alternative entertaining areas surrounded by low-maintenance garden beds.

The Solution

Designer Ken Parker was thrilled with Nathalie's large yard because it meant he could create a few distinct areas for entertaining, but still leave room for the kids to play. He cleaned up the deck with a fresh coat of green paint and got rid of the toys around it. He moved the *chiminea* down into the yard, where it wouldn't be a fire hazard.

Carpenter Lorne Hogan created another focal point and entertaining area by constructing a gazebo. This unique project featured a recycled wire satellite dish as the top of the gazebo, making it a surefire conversation piece. This project reflected Ken's approach to gardening. He uses natural products, favors native plants and recycles whenever possible.

Finally, both the firepit area and the gazebo were surrounded by new garden beds filled with plants that offered year-round interest.

The Projects

- Natural remedy for powdery mildew disease
- Choosing plants for fall interest

The Budget

Plant materials	$ 865.00
Satellite dish, hardware	$ 90.00
Accessories—chairs, table, pots	$ 498.00
Carpentry (gazebo base)	$ 484.00
TOTAL (excluding paint)	**$1937.00**

AFTER: Cleaned up and classed up with several areas for entertaining, the yard now offers a reason to leave the deck and enjoy it.

BEFORE (inset): Untidy and underutilized, this yard was bare and boring.

The Plan

Natural Remedy for Powdery Mildew Disease

Powdery mildew is a common fungal disease that appears on many trees and plants. While it may not kill a plant outright, it will weaken it, making it susceptible to other problems and compromising its appearance.

A plant that has powdery mildew will develop whitish powdery spots on leaves, stems and flowers. The disease is most likely to attack in spring and fall when the weather is cool and humidity is high. Most powdery mildew develops as layers of the fungus on the plant's surface. Their spores are carried by wind and rain and can spread quickly. Excess water, extreme heat and direct sunlight are all effective in debilitating the spores.

To reduce the chance of the disease occurring, you can:

- plant in sunnier rather than shadier spots

- space plants out to allow aeration and give them enough room to grow
- provide the proper amount of moisture for your plants.

If you do find a plant in your yard suffering from powdery mildew, treat it quickly. Ken Parker used the following natural remedy for this troublesome disease to treat a Canadian Serviceberry (*Amelanchier canadensis*).

Canadian Serviceberry

Materials you will need:

- 1 tbsp. (15 mL) baking soda
- 4 cups (1 L) water
- 3 drops dish soap
- Plastic spray bottle

1. Add baking soda to water.
2. Stir mixture and pour into plastic spray bottle.
3. Add three drops of dish soap to mixture.
4. Spray onto affected leaves, stems and flowers. Repeat weekly as needed.

DESIGN PLAN

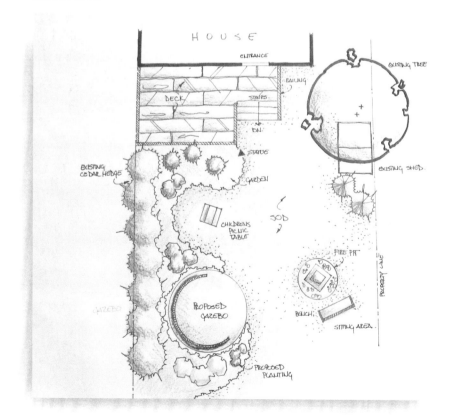

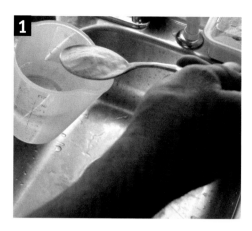

Choosing Plants for Fall Interest

Fall is a season of change. Dramatic color variations occur when the pinks, blues and whites of summer are pushed aside to make way for the yellows, oranges and reds of fall. Most gardeners associate these colors with foliage; however, there are some wonderful flowering plants at this time of year that combine well with the glowing foliage dangling overhead.

Ken chose to use a combination of plants in the Malettes' garden that would provide both flower and foliage interest in fall. Since Nathalie was a busy woman, Ken also chose low-maintenance plants that wouldn't take up too much of her time.

- **Virginia Sweetspire (*Itea virginica* 'Henry's Garnet')** is a versatile shrub that tolerates most soil conditions and a sunny or shaded location. It is hardy in USDA Zones 5-9 and reaches up to 4 feet (1.2 m) tall and 5 feet (1.5 m) wide. It produces spikes of fragrant white flowers in late summer, and its oblong green leaves turn a brilliant reddish-purple in fall. This easy-to-grow plant can be planted at any time and is ideal for mass or informal groupings.

- **Black-Eyed Susan Vine (*Thunbergia alata* 'Sunny Lemon Star')** is a trailing or twining annual vine that likes full sun to partial shade and moist, compost-enriched soil. It has triangular green leaves and masses of tubular yellow flowers with dark contrasting centers. Flowering starts in summer and

Virginia Sweetspire

Black-Eyed Susan Vine

White Snakeroot

- **White Snakeroot (*Eupatorium rugosum*)** is another plant with striking fall colors. White Snakeroot is a fast-growing perennial that reaches heights of 5 feet (1.5 m) tall. It has green ovate leaves and produces small, fuzzy white blooms, that appear as early as July and continue through to October. It likes rich, moist soils and sun or partial shade. It is hardy in USDA Zones 4-8.

continues well into October. This rapid grower reaches heights of up to 6 feet (2 m) tall. It can be used as a groundcover, in hanging baskets or trained on a trellis.

Just Say No!

Gardeners are becoming more ecologically aware of what they are putting into their gardens. Chemicals should always be a last resort when dealing with insects or diseases, as there are many natural weapons to choose from.

Gardening naturally will save time, money and, of course, the environment. Using natural materials increases the biological diversity of your soil. Healthy, vital soil is essential to growing plants, as healthy plants are more resistant to pests and diseases.

Here are some green ideas to use in your garden.

- To ensure that your soil is healthy, do a pH test to find out if you have acidic, alkaline or neutral soil. A test will also determine whether your soil is nutrient-deficient. Adding compost is a great way to bring nutrients to your garden and you can never add too much!
- For a healthy, chemical-free lawn, aerate it in the spring. You can rent an aerator or put on golf shoes and walk around. The spikes create small holes that increase oxygen penetration and improve drainage. Also, use a de-thatching rake in the fall to remove compacted grass stems and roots.

- Try the following natural remedies to rid your garden of pests:
- **Slugs:** a bowl of beer set in the garden; they can't resist!

- **Caterpillars:** Mix 1 tbsp (15 mL) molasses with 4 cups (1 L) of water; spray on plants.
- **Aphids:** Plant nasturtiums, garlic and chives to help repel aphids.

- **Flies & Mosquitoes:** Plant basil around patios to keep these pests away.
- **Nematodes:** Plant marigolds in your vegetable garden to help repel nematodes. Chives and onions also repel unwanted guests from your vegetable garden.

- **Weeds:** Mix 4 cups (1 L) of vinegar, 1 cup (60 mL) of salt and 2 tablespoons (30 mL) of dish soap; spray on weeds. Repeat as needed.

Other Plants

The Malettes' north-facing yard was a combination of sun and shade, so Ken had a range of options for the plants he could utilize.

- **Dwarf Ninebark (*Physocarpus opulifolius* 'Nanus')** is a dense shrub that likes full sun to part shade and tolerates a variety of soils. It produces white flowers in late spring and red fruit, and it has peeling orange bark that creates winter interest. It reaches heights of 4 feet (1.2 m) and is hardy in USDA Zones 3-7.

Dwarf Ninebark

- **Foamy Bells (*Heucherella* 'Sunspot')** is a hybrid of coral bells and foam flower, taking the best traits of each plant. It forms a low mound of chartreuse-yellow leaves with beet-red markings. Short spiky pink flowers appear in early summer. It does best in partial sun and moist soil. It has a moderate growth rate, reaching heights of 16 inches (40.6 cm) and a spread of 18 inches (45.7 cm). Hardy in USDA Zones 4-9.

Foamy Bells

■ **Palm-Branched Sedge (*Carex muskingumensis*)** is a perennial grasslike plant that is extremely hardy and adaptable. It is commonly called palm sedge because it resembles a miniature palm tree. Its green foliage turns yellow after the first frost. It thrives in full sun to partial shade and likes moist to wet soil. It is hardy in USDA Zones 5-9. It reaches heights of up to 20 inches (51 cm).

Nathalie Malette's gamble paid off. The space was classed-up when Ken and company transformed this garden into an elegant area for entertaining and relaxing, while still leaving plenty of room for child's play. The beds around the deck and gazebo were filled with low-maintenance plants that would give Nathalie and her family enjoyment year-round, without taking up too much time or energy. All that was left to do was light a fire and enjoy!

Palm-Branched Sedge

Safety First

An outdoor fireplace or *chiminea* is a great way to add a cozy touch to your garden. It will bring you hours of enjoyment, but remember these important safety tips:

1. Make sure your location is fire resistant and free from dry leaves and other combustible items. Also make sure there is nothing overhead such as branches, awnings, tents or canopies.
2. Never leave a fire unattended, even if it is covered.
3. Never leave children unsupervised around the fireplace.
4. Only put dry fuel, such as firewood or burning logs, into your fireplace.
5. Always have a water source close by in case of emergency.
6. Make sure your fire is completely out before you leave it.
7. Check the local fire codes in your area for more specific regulations.

Zone Map

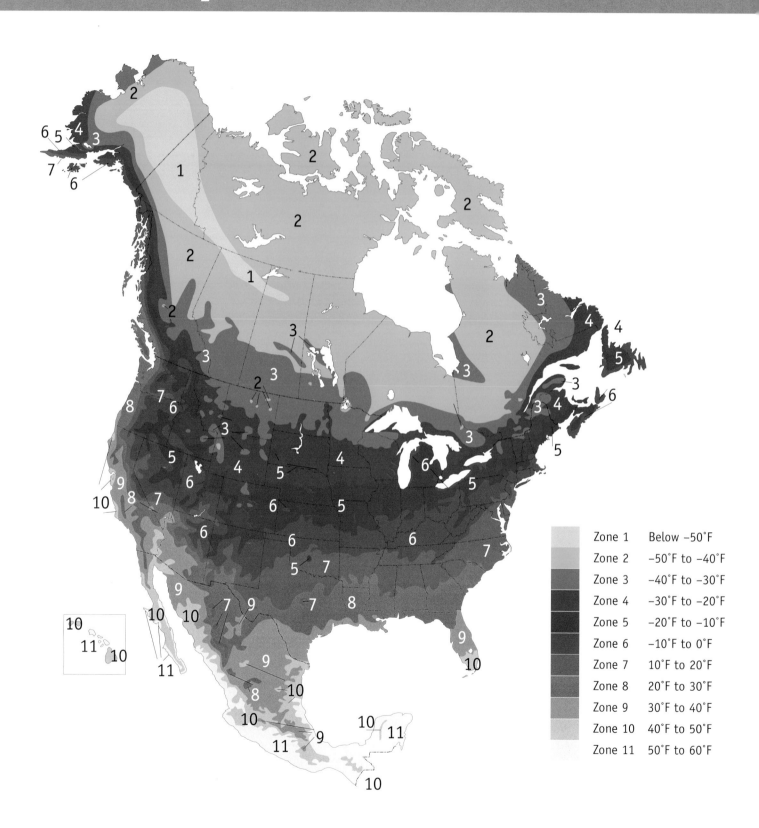

Zone 1	Below −50°F
Zone 2	−50°F to −40°F
Zone 3	−40°F to −30°F
Zone 4	−30°F to −20°F
Zone 5	−20°F to −10°F
Zone 6	−10°F to 0°F
Zone 7	10°F to 20°F
Zone 8	20°F to 30°F
Zone 9	30°F to 40°F
Zone 10	40°F to 50°F
Zone 11	50°F to 60°F

Range of average annual minimum temperature for each zone.

Glossary of Terms

Accent Plant
A plant positioned as a focal point or to catch attention.

Acidic Soil. *See* **pH**

Aerate
Digging up soil manually or with a machine to create air pockets.

Aggregate Culture
The use of solid material—such as gravel, rock wool or sand—in which to grow plants. All require the addition of a nutrient-rich water-soluble solution.

Alkaline Soil. *See* **pH**

Amendment. *See* **Soil Amendment**

Amphibious
The ability of some plants to grow both in water and in soil exposed to the air, usually in moist or boggy conditions as winter recedes.

Annual
A plant that grows, flowers and dies in one season.

Aphids
Small sap-sucking insects. They infect foliage and are easily recognized by the sugary "honey dew" they secrete that often attracts ants. Can be controlled by spraying with a solution of insecticidal soap and by other means.

Aquatic Plant
A plant that grows partially or completely in water.

Arbor
A freestanding structure used to support vines or climbing plants to provide shade, a walkway or a focal point. The term is often used interchangeably with "pergola."

Backfilling
Replacing soil from the original hole after planting.

Balled-and-Burlapped
A form in which plants are sold. The roots are wrapped in burlap or plastic-covered material to keep them together until transplanted. Large trees are often sold this way.

Bare-Root
Refers to shrubs and trees and sometimes perennials that are sold without soil around the roots.

Bearded
A flower petal bearing a tuft or row of long hairs.

Bedding Plants
Plants suitable for massing in beds for their colorful flowers or foliage. Usually annuals.

Bicolor
A flower with petals that bear two distinctly different colors.

Biodegradable
Capable of being decomposed by bacteria or other living organisms.

Biological Pest Control
Using living organisms such as beneficial insects or parasites to destroy garden pests.

Black Spot
A fungal disease that affects the foliage of plants, usually roses. It is caused by dampness. Plant disease resistant roses when possible, and clean tools after pruning. Spray affected plants with neem-tree oil, a fungicide or a baking-soda-and-water solution of one teaspoon (5 mL) to a quart (1 L) of water.

Botanical Name. *See* **Names of Plants**

Bract
Modified leaves growing just below a flower. Often confused with the flower itself.

Bud
The early stages of the development of a flower or leaf.

Building Code
Local rules, regulations and laws determining how structures can be made and by whom.

Bulb
A fleshy underground plant structure that contains the nutrients to produce a plant. Bulbs are usually planted underground at least one season before they emerge. Tulips and daffodils grow from bulbs.

Climatic Zones. *See* **Hardiness Zones**

Clay Soil
Soil with a high proportion of clay particles and small air pockets. Water retention is high, creating poor drainage.

Common Name. *See* **Names of Plants**

Compaction
Compaction is created by heavy machinery that squeezes the layers of soil together. It is destructive to the composition of the soil, removing air space, which plant roots need. The soil is also difficult to work with.

Companion Planting
Planting particular plants near one another so that one or more of them can benefit from the association. For example, nasturtiums help ward off some garden pests, as does garlic.

Compost
Decomposed garden waste—grass clippings, fallen leaves and other organic matter such as kitchen waste, although it's not a good idea to put meat leftovers in a composter; animals will invade.

Conifer
A cone-bearing tree, usually evergreen.

Container Gardening
Growing plants in containers (flowerpots or other suitable containers) rather than in a garden plot.

Creeper
A plant that sends out long shoots and grows along the ground. Ivy, Creeping Fig and Virginia Creeper are examples.

Crown
The point at which a plant's roots and stem join, usually at soil level.

Cultivar. *See* **Names of Plants**

Cultivate
To grow plants: planting, removing weeds and debris and loosening soil, etc.

Cut Back
To trim or cut a plant moderately in order to clean it up and encourage new growth.

Deadhead
To remove dead flowerheads to promote new blooms and improve the look of the plant.

Deciduous
Plants that naturally lose their leaves for the winter.

Decomposition
The decaying or breaking down of organic materials until they are no longer recognizable.

Dethatching
Removing dead grass and stems from lawn grass.

Division
A method of propagating plants by dividing into two or more sections and replanting separately.

Dormant Period
The time when a plant has naturally—and temporarily—stopped growing, usually in winter. Most perennials, trees and shrubs require it.

Drainage
The movement of water on land, either on the ground or underground.

Dwarf
A smaller variety of a particular plant.

Edging Plants
Compact plants that can be used to form a border.

Evergreens
Plants that retain their leaves year-round.

Everlasting
Flowers grown for drying for decorative purposes. Some plants are more suitable for this than others.

Exotic
Strictly speaking, a plant that is not native to the area, but popularly, it refers to any unusual or striking plant.

Family
A group of plants more broadly related than those in a genus (*see also* Names of Plants). Rosaceae (the rose family), for example, includes roses, some fruit trees and a great many other plants.

Fertilization
Giving plants nutrients so that they will

grow well. Also, pollination: When pollen from the anther (male part) of a plant reaches the stamen (female part) of the same or another compatible plant, the result is a seed.

Fibrous Root

A root system in which the roots are finely divided.

Forcing

Forcing a plant or a branch to bloom in an artificial environment—as spring bulbs are sometimes forced to bloom indoors out of season.

Frost

The condensation and freezing of moisture in the air when the temperature falls below the freezing point. First and last frost dates are important to know for your area because many plants are frost-sensitive.

Full Shade

A place that receives no direct sunlight.

Full Sun

A place that receives more than five hours of direct sun per day.

Fungicide

A chemical used to control fungal diseases.

Fungus

A form of plant life known to gardeners as one of the most common causes of plant diseases such as powdery mildew.

Genus. *See* **Names of Plants**

Germination

Sprouting. The earliest development of seedlings from seeds.

Grade

The degree of a slope. Also, the soil level in relation to another structure.

Groundcover

A creeping plant used to provide a low-growing carpet.

Growing Season

The time between the last frost date in spring and the first frost date in fall.

Habit

The shape or form of a plant, whether it grows vertically, laterally or rounded. It is useful to know the habits of plants when planning a garden.

Habitat

The environment in which a plant is usually found growing—and prefers. The main factors are climate and soil. Microclimates also play a part.

Hardiness

The ability of a plant to withstand low temperatures without protection.

Hardiness Zones

The division of North America into numbered zones based on average temperatures. The zone map produced by the U.S. Department of Agriculture is very useful for gardeners.

Hardscape

Any garden feature that is not a plant—decks, fences, benches, patios, etc.

Hedge

Suitable trees or shrubs planted fairly close together so that, as they grow, the branches will intertwine to provide a barrier for a windbreak or privacy.

Heirloom plants

Types of plants that have existed for 50 years or more.

Herbaceous

Describes a plant with a non-woody stem. Usually refers to perennials that die back to the ground in winter.

Herbicide

A chemical that kills plants.

Herbs

Aromatic plants used in cooking or for medicinal purposes.

Horticulture

The art and science of gardening.

Humus

Brown or black decomposed plant and animal material that forms the organic part of soil.

Hybrid

A hybrid is the result of cross-fertilization between different species or genera. Hybrids rarely produce seeds that will duplicate the parent plant. Some hybrids are sterile and do not reproduce at all.

Insecticide

A chemical that kills insects.

Invasive

The ability of a plant to spread quickly and crowd out other plants.

Japanese Gardens

Gardens designed with a Japanese cultural influence. Bamboo, pine, mondo grasses and koi fish are often used.

Landscape Architect

A very good professional to consult when creating a garden. He or she knows the mechanics of major construction, grading and drainage and will provide advice for solving problems.

Landscape Fabric

A synthetic material that blocks light, soil and weeds from penetrating but allows water to pass through. Also known as weed cloth.

Loam

The best garden soil—a balanced combination of clay, sand and organic matter.

Manure

Organic matter excreted by animals that, once decomposed, makes a wonderful fertilizer. Often sold bagged.

Marginal Plant

A plant that will grow on the edges of ponds or lakes and, when cultivated, will grow well around a water garden.

Mass Planting

The close planting of many of the same kind or color of flower to create a dramatic look.

Microclimate

A plant's immediate environment, which can be affected by nearby conditions and structures.

Mildew

Several different types of fungi. Two common types are downy and powdery mildew, which leave a white coating on leaves.

Mulch

A covering for soil that retains moisture, maintains temperature and prevents erosion and weeds. Mulch can be a natural or synthetic material.

Names of Plants. *See also* **Family; Hybrid**

Plant names are more complicated than in the following information, but at the level at which they are of interest to most gardeners, plants can have up to five different kinds of names:

• *Common names* for a given plant can be many and varied, depending on region, historical background, etc. Often, quite different plants have the same common name (bluebells, for example), which can be confusing. However, *botanical names* (see below), the result of a scientific classification system, clearly distinguish one plant from another, which common names do not. They also show relationships between plants that are not evident from the common names.

• The *genus name* (plural "genera") is part of the botanical name of a plant. It represents a group of closely related plants with different characteristics, rather like a human surname. The genus name is Latin-like and should be written in italics. The first letter is capitalized. *Brassica*, for example, is the genus name for a number of common food plants (broccoli, cauliflower, kohlrabi, etc.). Sometimes the genus name has become the common name of a plant as well. *Hosta*, *Impatiens* and *Hydrangea* are examples. When used as common names, they are usually not italicized or capitalized.

• *Species names* identify particular plants within a given genus. They are also written in italics but in lower case, and they follow the genus name. Red maple is *Acer rubrum*, and silver maple is *Acer saccharinum*, for example. Both belong to the genus *Acer*, but the species names are different because the trees are not quite the same.

• Some plants have a *variety name* as well. It can refer to a natural or human-bred version of a plant. Names of natural varieties or subspecies are also italicized.

• A *cultivar* (*culti*vated *variety*) is a human-bred version of a plant. It usually has some features that the natural version does not. When written, the cultivar name is *not* italicized, but the first letter of each word is capitalized, and it is enclosed in single quotation marks. Example: *Hydrangea paniculata* 'Tardiva,' which could also appear as 'Tardiva' hydrangea or some similar variation.

Native Plant

Any plant that occurs and grows naturally in a particular place.

Nitrogen
An essential nutrient for plant growth. On fertilizer packages, it is the N in N-P-K.

Nutrients
The substances a plant needs for growth and development.

Organic
Derived naturally from living or once-living plants or animals.

Partial Shade
Describes a garden that gets less than five hours of direct sunlight per day.

Pea Gravel
Gravel about the size of a pea. Frequently used in driveways, walkways and patios.

Peat Moss
Partially decomposed mosses that are used as a soil conditioner. It can also be a major ingredient in potting soil because it increases moisture retention. Sometimes used to line hanging planters.

Perennial
A plant that grows and flowers for many years. Some are evergreens; others (herbaceous perennials) die back to the ground in winter but will grow back again the following season.

Pergola
A freestanding structure with a roof or canopy designed to cast shade.

pH
The measurement of the soil's alkalinity or acidity on a scale of 1-14. A pH of 7 is neutral, 1-6 is acidic and 8-14 is alkaline.

Phosphorus
An essential nutrient for plant growth. On fertilizer packages it is the P in N-P-K.

Pinching
Using your thumb and forefinger to pinch off the tip growth of plants to encourage bushier growth. Also used in deadheading.

Pollen
Fine powdery yellowish grains that fertilize flowering plants.

Potassium
An essential nutrient for plant growth that promotes root growth and disease resistance. On fertilizer packages, it is the K in N-P-K.

Potting Soil
A soil mixture designed for use for potted plants. Potting mixes should be loose, light and sterile.

Propagation
Producing multiple plants from a single plant by various means (seeds, division, layering, etc.).

Pruning
Cutting off leaves or branches to remove dead or diseased foliage or branches. Also used to control or direct growth and to increase quality or yield of flowers or fruit.

Raised Beds
Planting areas that are mounded or boxed above ground level. Hilling soil is another method of raising the soil level. Raised soil dries out and warms up much more quickly in spring, permitting earlier planting.

Retaining Wall
A structure used to hold back soil, usually to create a level area in front of or behind the wall.

Rhizome
A horizontal fleshy stem on or under the ground that sends out both roots and new shoots.

Rock Garden
A garden area constructed of large rocks arranged to look natural and planted with plants that generally do not need a lot of care.

Rootball
The roots of a plant and the soil surrounding them.

Root Rot
Common in plants affected by fungal diseases. Poor drainage and overwatering can cause it.

Runner. *See also* **Stolon**

Stolon
A creeping stem that produces rootlets along its length.

Sandy Soil
Soil with a high percentage of sand or large soil particles. Water retention is low, and nutrients leach out quickly.

Scale
A design element. Refers to the size of an object in relation to its surroundings.

Screen
A structure or planting that blocks a view or another structure.

Shrub
A woody plant with a framework of branches and little or no central stem, unlike a tree, which has a main trunk.

Soil Amendment
Soil additives, usually organic, that contribute nutrients and texture to the soil and balance the pH.

Soil Test
A process by which the nutrients and pH of soil are determined. Test your soil before amending it.

Species. *See* **Names of Plants**

Sphagnum Moss. *See* **Peat Moss**

Stem
The main trunk of a plant that develops buds and shoots.

Stolon. *See also* **Runner**
A shoot that runs along the ground, takes root and produces a new plant at its tip.

Succulent
Succulent plants have thick, fleshy leaves or stems (or both). They often have waxy

outer layers as well. These adaptations allow the plants to retain water well.

Tendril
Some climbing plants such as sweet peas, clematis and grapes produce a cordlike structure that enables them to grasp a supportive structure.

Texture
A design element that is both tactile and visual.

Thatch
A layer of dead grass that builds up between the soil level and lawn grass blades. It prevents air, water and fertilizer from reaching the roots.

Topsoil
Top layer of soil.

Transplant
To move a plant from one area or pot to another.

Trellis
A structure that climbing plants can grow on, either freestanding or attached to a wall.

Tropical Plant
A plant that grows naturally in a tropical area. Many plants used as annuals in the north are tropical (impatiens, for example, which is a perennial in its home environment).

Tuber
A round, underground mass of plant tissue that is the source of new growth. Potatoes are tubers.

Variegated
A plant with leaves that are striped, blotched, edged or spotted with another color, usually yellow, white or cream.

Variety. *See* **Names of Plants**

Vermiculite
Mica, a mineral that is heated and puffed up to form lightweight, sponge-like granules capable of holding both water and air. Often used in potting-soil combinations.

Water Garden
Any human-made pool or container in which aquatic plants are planted.

Weed
An uninvited plant, usually one that grows vigorously.

Wildflower
A plant that grows without human intervention in its native environment. Weeds are wildflowers, although some wildflowers do not come to one's garden uninvited.

Xeriscaping
Cultivation of gardens using a variety of techniques in order to reduce the need for water.

About the Show

*T*he *Gardening Gamble* is reality TV with a green twist. Two sets of friends or families give up control of their gardens and switch homes for the weekend. Each team gets a landscape designer and a carpenter, a budget of $2,000 and two days to transform each other's space. Not only do they not know what is going to happen to their yard, they don't have ANY say. . . that's the "Gamble!"

The Gardening Gamble results are often unpredictable. . . and it's not always roses and white picket

fences! But viewers can always count on tips, tricks and easy-to-follow projects that they can apply to their own spaces—and now, not just from the show, but from *The Gardening Gamble* book as well! We hope you'll discover that just because the budget is practical, it doesn't mean the results can't be grand! That's *The Gardening Gamble* philosophy. And now you too can learn how to put that philosophy into practice!

Biographies

John-Mark Bouwmeister
Cedarock Landscaping Inc./*Greener Senses*
Landscape Designer

- *Surf 'n' Turf*
- *Drive-Through Garden*

As a child, John was often found playing in the dirt or damming up local creeks to create waterfalls. Many generations of great gardeners preceded him, so John has his work cut out. "I really enjoy working in the landscape industry . . . . I think I may have more kilometers on my wheelbarrow than I do on my truck."

John currently owns and operates Cedarock Landscaping and *Greener Senses* magazine.

Christopher Chung
CMC Contracting
Landscape Designer

- *East Meets West*

Christopher Chung, owner and operator of CMC Contracting, graduated from Concordia University, Liberal Arts College and film studies. His interest in Asian culture, aesthetics and philosophy influences his designs, from the minimalism of Zen Buddhism to the rustic Japanese Tea Garden. His approach to landscaping is characterized by a unique combination of art, meditative activity and cultural experience. In creating a harmonious environment, one can be physically and spiritually connected to the world.

Michael Didulka
Didulka, Young & Associates
Certified Landscape Designer

- *A Work of Art*
- *Stone-Age Garden*
- *Kinder-Garden*

With two decades of experience in the landscape profession, Toronto-born Michael Didulka is a principal of Didulka, Young & Associates, an innovative, multidisciplinary landscaping firm, offering creative planning and design services to commercial, industrial and residential clientele.

"I'm committed to marrying architecture with the environment in the creation of designs that are functional and aesthetically pleasing," says Michael.

Michael is an Associate Member of the Ontario Association of Landscape Architects (OALA) and a graduate of Ryerson Polytechnic University's

Landscape Architecture program.

In his spare time, Michael can be found in front of his computer or drafting table, creating landscaping plans for family, friends and television.

Beth Edney, CLD
Designs by the Yard Inc.
Certified Landscape Designer

- *Patio Pick-Me-Up*
- *Message in a Bottle*
- *Garden in a Jiffy*
- *All Decked Out*
- *A Tier-ful Garden*

Beth is a Certified Landscape Designer. She has been running her own landscape design firm, Designs By the Yard Inc., for over 10 years. She is an active member of Landscape Ontario. Her work has been featured on HGTV, W Network and in numerous publications such as *Chatelaine, Reader's Digest,* the *Toronto Star* and the

Toronto Sun. Beth's background education is in art and architecture, as well as landscape architecture. Her gardens are always unique, as she tries to reflect the homeowner's personality and lifestyle in her designs.

Edgar Friars
Edgarden
Landscape Designer

- ■ *Color My Garden*
- ■ *A Hair-Raising Gothic Garden*

Since he was a toddler, horticulturist Edgar Friars has been fascinated with garden design, and when he grew up, he became assistant manager for Weall and Cullen Nurseries Ltd.—a career that lasted almost 10 years. Today, he's a certified horticulture technician and produces the *Mark Cullen Garden Show* on Canada's Newstalk 1010 CFRB radio. He is also a frequent contributor to the television series *Earth Alive* (Rogers Cable). In addition to his radio and television gigs, Edgar is a technician at Toronto's prestigious boys' school, Upper Canada

College. Edgar says that his years of training and experience help him bring his unique flair to the landscape industry.

Rena Hans
Camilla House Imports
Designer

- ■ *A Formal Affair*
- ■ *A Rose-Colored Garden*
- ■ *A Call to Order*
- ■ *A Garden that Soars to New Heights*

Rena Hans manages and designs for the leading wholesale Home and Garden furniture outlet, Camilla House Imports. The company designs and manufactures a range of home-and-garden furniture and accessories that are carried across North America. It is a Canadian company with showrooms in Toronto, Atlanta, New York and High Point.

Rena manages the product development and marketing arm of the company and is instrumental in choosing and sourcing out new products from various suppliers in Vietnam, China, Indonesia, the Philippines and India.

Traveling twice a year to various trade shows in

Europe and the Far East exposes Rena to upcoming trends in the market— and she tries to incorporate these trends in the designs that she does on *The Gardening Gamble*.

Cathy Merklinger
PAYDIRT Designs
Landscape Designer

- ■ *A Shady Deal*
- ■ *Sunstroke*

Cathy Merklinger is a "designing" lady with a fine arts background from the University of Waterloo. She first pursued designing as a florist for Weall and Cullen Nurseries for 10 years. Her love of plants led her to head back to school and earn her a Certificate of Landscape Design from Ryerson Polytechnic University. She worked for several years as a landscape designer with Sheridan Nurseries before venturing out on her own. Her design company PAYDIRT Designs specializes in creating elegant, functional "sanctuaries" for urban homeowners. When Cathy is not gardening or designing, she enjoys jazz music, traveling, playing tennis, hiking, kayaking,

dance, swimming and reading. A husband, two teenage daughters, a dog, a cat, fish and a hamster keep her spare time filled with laughter and fun!

Ken Parker
Linda Parker
Sweet Grass Gardens
Landscape Designers

- ■ *DISHing the Dirt*
- ■ *Pardon My Garden*

Ken and Linda Parker are co-owners of Sweet Grass Gardens, North America's first Native-owned and operated native plant nursery. Retail operations are located on Six Nations of the Grand River First Nation in Ontario, Canada. The Aboriginal couple has spent the past decade diligently working to restore, preserve and maintain pre-European plant species indigenous to North America. Their mission is "to preserve the history of North America and its First Nation people by encouraging the rediscovery and respect for our traditional Mother Earth." Their philosophy and gardening approach is simple —let the site dictate the plant material. Selecting the appropriate plant material for the space and hardiness zone will reduce plant stress, minimize watering and encourage a chemical-free natural garden for wildlife to enjoy.

Jennifer Reynolds
Jennifer Reynolds & Associates, Inc.
Landscape Designer

■ *The Outback*

Jennifer Reynolds is a landscape designer and passionate organic gardener. Over her 16 years of experience in the gardening industry, she has worked in garden center retail, is a four-time award-winning landscape designer, a floral designer, a garden writer and editor and a guest speaker at home and gardening events. Jennifer sits on the Board of Directors at the Toronto Botanical Garden and is an enthusiastic volunteer within the organization.

The Carpenters

Lorne Hogan

This part-time actor/full-time carpenter has owned and operated Canadian Classic Contracting for over six years. Lorne says he enjoys working on *The Gardening Gamble* because it gives him the opportunity to combine his love of hands-on work with meeting new people. New to us during our second season, Lorne has proved to be a fun and energetic addition to the crew. Reflecting on his contracting business, Lorne reminds us to choose a job you like, and you'll never work a day in your life! He says *The Gardening Gamble* fits the definition of what a "fun job" should be.

Christopher Pinkerton

Chris Pinkerton has owned and operated his contracting company, Overall Renovations, for 20 years. Married, with two beautiful children, Kai and Carly, Chris enjoys being able to turn a client's renovation dream into reality. He loves to use his hands as well as play with power tools and says *The Gardening Gamble* allows him the opportunity to explore the creative side of carpentry.

Jordan Taylor

Jordan, 1991 graduate of Ryerson's Radio and Television Arts Program—is a self-proclaimed thrill seeker and world traveller. She's lived in five different countries, including the Cayman Islands where a large part of her broadcasting career unfolded.

One of the highlights of Jordan's career happened while working abroad, when she witnessed and reported on history in the making. She did live telephone broadcasts from South Africa to the Cayman Islands as Nelson Mandela was elected the first black president of his country. The experience, she says, was unforgettable.

Since returning to Canada in 2001, Jordan has hosted television specials and appeared in numerous commercials and voice overs. In addition to her hosting duties on W's new series, *The Gardening Gamble,* Jordan is also a news anchor at 680 News.

Jordan also keeps herself busy by trying new things including parasailing, scubadiving, hot-air ballooning and white water rafting. But, perhaps, her biggest adventure was shooting *The Gardening Gamble.*

George Tsiotsioulas

George is no stranger to television. For the past seven years he's produced and hosted *Nite Life*—an entertainment segment—for CFMT Television in Toronto. On the series, he's interviewed some of North America's hottest celebrities including David Bowie, Britney Spears, Oasis, Kevin Spacey, and Sally Field, to name a few.

When he's not working, he loves to travel. Some of his favourite destinations include Hong Kong, Denmark, Cuba and Venezuela. Being of Greek descent, Greece holds a special place in his heart, and he tries to visit friends and family there as much as possible.

While work and play keep him busy, George also knows how to enjoy his down time and says he loves writing poetry and short stories. He's also a music fan and jokes, "I've sung in a few bands over the years, but my dream of becoming a rock star is currently on hold!"

His life may be hectic but George says, "I'm always up for new challenges . . . I believe that you should fill your life with as many interesting experiences as possible."

Co-hosting *The Gardening Gamble* has been an experience he'll never forget!